The Recovery
of the Church

The
Holy
Word
for
Morning
Revival

Watchman Nee
Witness Lee

Living Stream Ministry
Anaheim, CA • www.lsm.org

First Edition, October 2017.

ISBN 978-0-7363-8920-4

Published by

Living Stream Ministry
2431 W. La Palma Ave., Anaheim, CA 92801 U.S.A.
P. O. Box 2121, Anaheim, CA 92814 U.S.A.

Printed in the United States of America

17 18 19 / 4 3 2 1

International Training for Elders and
Responsible Ones—
October 2017

THE RECOVERY OF THE CHURCH

Contents

Preface

1. This book is intended as an aid to believers in developing
a daily time of morning revival with the Lord in His word.
At the same time, it provides a limited review of the
International Training for Elders and Responsible Ones
held in Leipzig, Germany, on October 5-7, 2017. The general subject of the training was "The Recovery of the
Church." Through intimate contact with the Lord in His
word, the believers can be constituted with life and truth
and thereby equipped to prophesy in the meetings of the
church unto the building up of the Body of Christ.

2. The book is divided into weeks. One training message is
covered per week. Each week presents first the message
outline, followed by six daily portions, a hymn, and then
some space for writing. The message outline has been
divided into days, corresponding to the six daily portions.
Each daily portion covers certain points and begins with
a section entitled "Morning Nourishment." This section
contains selected verses and a short reading that can
provide rich spiritual nourishment through intimate fellowship with the Lord. The "Morning Nourishment" is
followed by a section entitled "Today's Reading," a longer
portion of ministry related to the day's main points. Each
day's portion concludes with a short list of references for
further reading and some space for the saints to make
notes concerning their spiritual inspiration, enlightenment, and enjoyment to serve as a reminder of what they
have received of the Lord that day.

3. The space provided at the end of each week is for compos-
ing a short prophecy. This prophecy can be composed by
considering all of our daily notes, the "harvest" of our inspi-
rations during the week, and preparing a main point with
some sub-points to be spoken in the church meetings for
the organic building up of the Body of Christ.

4. Following the last week in this volume, we have provided
reading schedules for both the Old and New Testaments in
the Recovery Version with footnotes. These schedules are

arranged so that one can read through both the Old and New Testaments of the Recovery Version with footnotes in two years.

5. As a practical aid to the saints' feeding on the Word throughout the day, we have provided verse cards at the end of the volume, which correspond to each day's Scripture reading. These may be cut out and carried along as a source of spiritual enlightenment and nourishment in the saints' daily lives.

6. The content of this book is taken primarily from the published training outlines, the text and footnotes of the Recovery Version of the Bible, selections from the writings of Witness Lee and Watchman Nee, and *Hymns,* all of which are published by Living Stream Ministry.

7. The training message outlines were compiled by Living Stream Ministry from the writings of Witness Lee and Watchman Nee. The outlines, footnotes, and cross-references in the Recovery Version of the Bible are by Witness Lee. Unless otherwise noted, the references cited in this publication are by Witness Lee.

8. For the sake of space, references to *The Collected Works of Watchman Nee* and *The Collected Works of Witness Lee* are abbreviated to *CWWN* and *CWWL,* respectively.

International Training
for Elders and Responsible Ones
(October 2017)

General Subject:

The Recovery of the Church

Seeing God's Eternal Purpose
concerning the Church
and
Enlightening All
concerning the Economy of the Mystery
Hidden in God

Scripture Reading: Eph. 3:3-5, 8-11; Rom. 8:28; 16:25

Day 1   I. **In order to participate in the recovery of the church, we need to see God's eternal purpose concerning the church (Eph. 1:9, 11; 3:9-11; Rom. 8:28):**
   A. A purpose is a determined intent to do something or to gain something:
      1. The determined will of God became the purpose of God (Eph. 1:5).
      2. God's purpose is His determined intent to gain the church (vv. 9, 11).
   B. The eternal purpose (lit., "the purpose of the ages") was made by God in eternity past for eternity future (3:11):
      1. The purpose of the ages is the purpose of eternity, the eternal purpose.
      2. In eternity past, before the foundation of the world, before the heavens, the earth, and all things were created, God made a purpose for something in the future, in eternity to come; therefore, it is called the purpose of eternity, the eternal purpose (1:4-5, 9, 11; 3:11).
   C. The word *purpose* in Ephesians 3:11 is equivalent to the word *plan;* we may speak of the eternal plan which God planned in Christ:
      1. God has a plan, which He planned in eternity; God's eternal purpose is God's eternal plan.
Day 2   2. *His purpose* in Romans 8:28 refers to the purposeful determination in God's plan.
      3. God's plan is to have a corporate expression

of Himself in Christ the Son by the Spirit
through the Body composed and built up with
many regenerated and transformed people
by the mingling of Himself with humanity
(Eph. 1:22-23; 4:16).

D. Ephesians 3:10-11 reveals that the existence of
the church is according to the eternal purpose
which He made in Christ Jesus our Lord:

1. The church was planned by God in eternity;
before time began, in eternity, God purposed
to have the church (1:4-5, 9, 11, 22-23).

2. In eternity past and for eternity to come, God
planned and purposed to have the church in
Christ and for Christ (3:10-11):

   a. The church is not a temporary matter but
   an eternal matter in the eternal purpose
   of God; the church is the center and subject of God's eternal plan.

   b. God planned in eternity past to have the
   church, and He expects to have the church
   in eternity to come.

   c. The church is in this age and throughout this age, yet it is from eternity past
   and for eternity future (Matt. 16:18; 18:17;
   Rev. 21:2, 9-11).

E. God planned to have the church composed of
regenerated and transformed human beings who
are coordinated and built together as a corporate Body (Eph. 1:22-23; 2:21-22; 3:14-21):

1. God planned that this corporate Body would
be a corporate vessel into which He would
work Himself (vv. 14-17).

2. God's purpose, His determined intention, is to
have a corporate Body, a corporate vessel, with
which He could mingle Himself and all that
He has; this vessel is the church (4:4-6, 16).

3. The church is dear, lovable, and precious to
God because the church is His good pleasure, the desire of His heart (1:5, 9, 22-23).

Day 3   F. The existence of the universe is according to
                 God's eternal purpose to have the church (Rev.
                 4:11; Eph. 3:9-11):
                 1. The full revelation of the Scriptures unveils
                    to us that all things in the universe are for
                    the church (v. 9).
                 2. Even the three persons of the Godhead are
                    for the divine purpose of having the church
                    to fulfill God's eternal plan through the dis-
                    pensing of God in His Divine Trinity into
                    humanity so that the church may come into
                    existence (1:3-23; Matt. 28:19; 16:18; 2 Cor.
                    13:14; 1:1).
                 3. The heavens, the earth, a multitude of other
                    things, and the tripartite man are required
                    in order that the church may exist to ex-
                    press God; without these things God cannot
                    have the church in the universe to be His
                    corporate expression (Zech. 12:1; Rev. 4:11).

Day 4   G. God's intention concerning the church is three-
                 fold: to express Himself through the sonship (Eph.
                 1:5), to make His multifarious wisdom known to
                 the enemy (3:10), and to head up all things in
                 Christ (1:10).

          II. **We need "to enlighten all that they may see
              what the economy of the mystery is, which
              throughout the ages has been hidden in God,
              who created all things" (3:9):**
              A. The New Testament tells us that the church was
                 a mystery in God; throughout all the genera-
                 tions before the New Testament time, the church
                 was a mystery (vv. 3-6, 9; 5:32).
              B. In the Bible a mystery refers not only to things
                 that are hidden and unknown to us but also to
                 things that are hidden in God's heart; this is the
                 principle concerning the mysteries mentioned
                 in the Bible (Mark 4:11; Rom. 16:25-26; Col.
                 1:26-27; 2:2; 4:3; Eph. 1:9; 3:3-4, 9; 5:32; 6:19).

Day 5   C. God's mystery is His hidden purpose, which is to dispense Himself into His chosen people; hence, there is the economy of the mystery of God (3:9).

D. From the beginning of the world the purpose of creation was a mystery hidden in God; no one knew what the purpose of creation was (Rev. 4:11; Eph. 3:9; Col. 1:16):
  1. Job was right in saying, "You have hidden these things in Your heart: / I know that this is with You"; what was hidden in God's heart was the mystery of the ages (Job 10:13; Eph. 3:9).
  2. After creating man in His image and according to His likeness, God kept His intention hidden throughout the ages (Gen. 1:26; Rom. 16:25).
  3. Before the New Testament time God did not unveil to anyone what His purpose was; the mystery, God's hidden purpose, was made known by revelation to the apostles and prophets (Eph. 3:3-5).

E. The mystery hidden in God's heart is God's eternal economy (1:10; 3:9; 1 Tim. 1:4), which is God's eternal intention with His heart's desire to dispense Himself in His Divine Trinity as the Father in the Son by the Spirit into His chosen people to be their life and nature so that they may be the same as He is as His duplication (Rom. 8:29; 1 John 3:2), to become an organism, the Body of Christ as the new man (Eph. 2:15-16), for God's fullness, God's expression (1:22-23; 3:19), which will become the New Jerusalem (Rev. 21:2—22:5).

Day 6 F. In Ephesians 3:4 Paul uses the expression *the mystery of Christ* to explain the church as the Body of Christ in God's eternal economy, indicating that the church is the mystery of Christ.

G. The economy of God's mystery is to have the church for the manifestation of God (vv. 9-10).

H. Paul preached not only the gospel of the

unsearchable riches of Christ; he also preached
the gospel concerning the economy of the mystery hidden in God (vv. 8-9):

1. The gospel concerning the economy of the
   mystery hidden in God is to produce the church
   for God's expression and glorification according to God's eternal purpose (vv. 10-11, 21).

2. Today we must announce the gospel concerning the mystery hidden in God in order
   to enlighten all so that they may see what is
   the economy of the mystery hidden in God,
   who created all things for the fulfillment
   of His will, the desire of His heart, and His
   eternal purpose (1:5, 9, 11; 3:8-11).

Morning Nourishment

Eph. Even as He chose us in Him before the foundation
1:4 of the world to be holy and without blemish before
Him in love.

11 In whom also we were designated as an inheritance, having been predestinated according to the
purpose of the One who works all things according
to the counsel of His will.

Today the word "church" is very common. But when Paul
comes to the revelation of the church, he uses certain mysterious expressions. He calls the church a mystery, even a hidden
mystery. This mystery is hidden in God's household arrangement. In eternity past, God the Father had a household arrangement, and in that arrangement a mystery was hidden.

We need to look into the details concerning God's eternal economy. This economy is an eternal plan; it is also a purpose. In
Ephesians the word *purpose* is used three times, twice as a noun
(1:11; 3:11) and once as a verb (1:9). God is purposeful, and He has
a purpose. But what does the word *purpose* mean?...A purpose is
a strong intent to do something or to gain something. The eternal
economy of God is of God's determined intent, of God's purpose. In
eternity past God had such an intent to gain something, to have
something. God is determined to have the church. With a definite
and strong determination, God intends to have the church. (*The
Conclusion of the New Testament,* p. 2047)

Today's Reading

According to footnote 1 on Ephesians 3:11, God's eternal purpose is the purpose of the ages. The purpose of the ages is the purpose of eternity, the eternal purpose, the eternal plan of God made
in eternity past. Hence, the expression *the purpose of the ages,* a lit-
eral translation of the Greek, simply means the "eternal purpose."

Besides the terms *economy, mystery,* and *purpose,* a number
of other important terms are used by Paul in Ephesians. The
next term we shall consider is *will.* Three times in Ephesians 1
Paul speaks of God's will: the good pleasure of His will (v. 5), the

mystery of His will (v. 9), and the counsel of His will (v. 11). God has an economy because in eternity God had a will. Because this will was hidden in Him, it was a mystery. But in His wisdom and prudence God has made this hidden mystery known to us through His revelation in Christ, that is, through Christ's incarnation, crucifixion, resurrection, and ascension.

God's eternal, determined intent is to have something. This intent, this purpose, plan, and arrangement, household administration, is of God's will....God's will is the source, and the purpose is the outcome. God's eternal purpose is of His will.

What is the will which is the source of God's purpose, the source of God's determined intent? The simplest answer is that God's will is what God wants....Every living person has a will. As soon as a child is born, he wants something, and what the child wants is his will.

What does God want? God wants the church. God wants us for the church. The church is something of God's will, for the church is what God wants....His wanting to have the church is His will. Of this will God determined an intent, and this intent is His purpose. (*The Conclusion of the New Testament*, pp. 2047-2048)

The church is something of God's eternal plan, His eternal purpose. It is something planned by God in His eternal plan, something purposed by God in eternity and for eternity. Ephesians 3:10-11 gives us the scriptural ground to speak of the church as something of God's eternal purpose....[In verse 11], the Greek word for *purpose* means "plan." God has purposed a purpose, He planned a plan, and this purpose, this plan, is called the eternal purpose. In eternity past, before the foundation of this world, before the heavens, the earth, and all things were created, God made such a purpose for something in the future, in eternity to come. Therefore, it is called the purpose of eternity, the eternal purpose. (*Basic Principles for the Practice of the Church Life*, pp. 7-8)

Further Reading: Basic Principles for the Practice of the Church Life, ch. 1; *The Conclusion of the New Testament*, msg. 189

Enlightenment and inspiration: _____

_____

_____

_____

Morning Nourishment

Eph. In order that now to the rulers and the authorities
3:10-11 in the heavenlies the multifarious wisdom of God
might be made known through the church, according to the eternal purpose which He made in
Christ Jesus our Lord.

In order to share in the recovery of the proper church life, we
need to see what God's purpose was in the beginning. We need to
understand that there are three different beginnings. John 1:1
says, "In the beginning was the Word." The beginning here is the
beginning in eternity. Genesis 1:1 says, "In the beginning God
created the heavens and the earth." In this verse the beginning
denotes the time of creation. Finally, the beginning also refers to
the start of the church life. Therefore, to go back to the beginning
is to go back to the beginning in eternity, to the beginning in
God's creation, or to the beginning of the church. (*Life-study of
Ephesians*, p. 563)

Today's Reading

God's eternal purpose is God's eternal plan. God has a plan,
which He planned in eternity—He is not purposeless; He is a
God of purpose. (*CWWL, 1968*, vol. 1, "The Practical Expression
of the Church," p. 341)

["His purpose" in Romans 8:28 refers] to the purposeful
determination in God's plan. This is God's purpose to produce
many brothers of His firstborn Son. (Rom 8:28, footnote 5)

The church is a great matter; it was planned by God, and
strictly speaking it is the very economy of God for His plan.
God's economy is wholly related to the church. What God
planned and what He is operating to carry out is the church, so
the church is the very center of God's economy....In order to
understand the church, we must realize that it is the center of
God's plan and the very substance of His economy.

We may say that the aim of God's eternal purpose is to have
the church, but this is too general. If we study Ephesians with a
spirit of revelation, we will realize that the aim of God's plan is to

have an expression of Himself in Christ the Son by the Spirit through a Body composed and built up with many regenerated and transformed people by the mingling of Himself with humanity. (*CWWL, 1964*, vol. 2, "A General Sketch of the New Testament in the Light of Christ and the Church, Part 2—Romans through Philemon," p. 298)

Ephesians 3:10-11 unveils the fact that the existence of the church is according to the eternal purpose of God which He made in Christ....[The church] did not come into existence by accident but was planned in eternity. Before time began, in eternity, God purposed to have the church. (*CWWL, 1968*, vol. 1, "The Practical Expression of the Church," p. 341)

In eternity past and for eternity to come, God planned and purposed to have a church in Christ and for Christ. Therefore, the church is not a temporary matter but an eternal matter. The church is in this age and throughout this age, yet it is from eternity past and for eternity future. It is an eternal matter in the eternal purpose of God, and it is the center, the subject of God's eternal plan. (*Basic Principles for the Practice of the Church Life*, p. 8)

What did God plan? He planned to have a church composed of a group of human beings coordinated together as a corporate Body with which He may mingle Himself in His divine nature. In other words, this corporate Body would be a corporate vessel, into which He would put Himself. This is the very thing God planned, and this is the very center of His purpose. God planned to have a corporate Body, a corporate vessel, with which He could mingle Himself and all that He is. This vessel is called the church.

The church, therefore, is the center of God's eternal plan. Why is the church so dear, so lovable, and so precious to God? It is because the church is the desire of God's heart, which He purposed before time began. God in eternity planned to have the church. (*CWWL, 1968*, vol. 1, "The Practical Expression of the Church," p. 341)

Further Reading: CWWL, 1968, vol. 1, "The Practical Expression of the Church," ch. 1; *God's Plan concerning the Church*, chs. 1-3

Enlightenment and inspiration: _____

_____

_____

_____

Morning Nourishment

Rev. You are worthy, our Lord and God, to receive the
4:11   glory and the honor and the power, for You have
        created all things, and because of Your will they
        were, and were created.
2 Cor. The grace of the Lord Jesus Christ and the love of
13:14   God and the fellowship of the Holy Spirit be with
        you all.

God's good pleasure is the desire of His heart, that is, to have
the church, and God's revelation of His hidden will is according
to this desire of His heart. This is according to His good pleasure.

God's good pleasure has been purposed by God in Himself.
This means that God Himself is the initiation, origination, and
sphere of His eternal purpose....The existence of the universe is
according to God's purpose. Heaven, earth, millions of items, and
the human race are all according to God's purposed desire. Eventually, all these things will issue in God's desire....Because this
desire has been purposed by God, no one and nothing can over-
throw it. Everything that takes place on earth is for this purpose.
We, the sons of God, in whom God's grace abounds, are the focal
point of His purpose, and everything is working for us. God has
purposed this desire in Himself. He did not take counsel with anyone else regarding it. (*Life-study of Ephesians,* pp. 68-69)

Today's Reading

God's good pleasure is what He has purposed in Himself for
an administration (Eph. 1:10)....The Greek word rendered "administration" is *oikonomia,* from which we get the English
word *economy.* God has purposed to have an economy. All the
kingdoms in the universe—the angelic kingdom, the demonic
kingdom, the human kingdom, the animal kingdom, and the
plant kingdom—are for this economy, this administration, and
are moving toward it. (*Life-study of Ephesians,* p. 69)

The full revelation of the Scripture reveals to us that all
things in the universe are for the church. Even the three persons of the Godhead are for the divine purpose of having a

church to fulfill God's eternal plan.

We are all familiar with the three persons of the Godhead: God the Father, God the Son, and God the Spirit. These three persons of the Godhead do not exist so that we may have a doctrine of the Trinity but are for the accomplishment of God's plan to produce the church. They are for the dispensing of God Himself into humanity in order that the church may come into existence.

God the Father is the source of the heavenly electricity; God the Son is the current of the heavenly electricity; and God the Spirit is the application, the function, of the heavenly electricity. Thus, God Himself can be dispensed into us and applied so that the church may be produced and exist. For the producing and existence of the church, God must be in three persons.

In order that the church may exist in this universe to express God, the heavens, the earth, space, and a multitude of other items are required. Without these things God could never have a church in the universe to express Himself....Everything is for the church, and everything is because of the church.

For the producing of the church, there is also the need of a tripartite man, a man with three parts—spirit, soul, and body.... Not only is there the need of man, but of man in three parts, with a body, a soul, and a spirit. Why must man be in three parts? The body of man is related to the creation. The soul of man is related to man himself, and the spirit of man is related to God. Thus, there could be a church composed of man in the universe.

Without God in three persons, without the creation of so many things, and without man in three parts, it is impossible for the church to come into existence. For the purpose of having the church, all these are necessary. God, creation, and man are all for the church; so eventually we see that the church is the center, the kernel, of God's eternal plan. (*CWWL, 1968*, vol. 1, "The Practical Expression of the Church," pp. 341-343)

Further Reading: God's Purpose for the Church; Life-study of Ephesians, msg. 31

Enlightenment and inspiration: _____

_____

_____

_____

Morning Nourishment

Eph. And to enlighten all *that they may see* what the econ-
3:9 omy of the mystery is, which throughout the ages
has been hidden in God, who created all things.
5:32 This mystery is great, but I speak with regard to
Christ and the church.

I am still burdened to speak about God's purpose concerning
the church....Perhaps many of us have a little understanding,
but we may not have been brought into a full realization. Moreover, we should be able to speak the things we have heard and
minister what we have been impressed with.

There are three main items of God's purpose for the church.
The first is that the church must have the full sonship (Eph. 1:4-5).
The second is that God may show His wisdom to the enemy
through the church (3:9-11). Third, God's purpose is to head up
all things in Christ through the church (1:10, 21-23). This utter-
ance is brief, clear, effective, and full. In studying the book of
Ephesians, the verses cited above are the most difficult verses
for people to understand. Nevertheless, God's purpose with the
church is in these verses....The sonship, God's wisdom made
known, and the heading up of all things are the three main
items of God's purpose concerning the church. (*CWWL, 1965,*
vol. 1, "The Vision, Practice, and Building Up of the Church as
the Body of Christ," p. 63)

Today's Reading

Throughout all the generations before the New Testament
time, the church was a mystery. *Mystery* indicates that something was hidden that no one knew about. Do you know why God
created the heavens, the earth, and thousands and thousands of
items? Do you know why God created the race of Adam, the
human people? You need to answer this question by saying, "It
was to have the church." The intention, the desire, of God is not
to have heaven, not to have the earth, and not to have many different items. The intention, the desire, of God in this universe is
to have the church. Therefore, everything is for the church.

The heavens, the earth, and all things are for the church, but before the New Testament time God never told this to anyone. Adam did not know it, Abraham did not know it, Moses did not know it, and David did not know it. It was a mystery; no one in the Old Testament times ever knew it. Is this still a mystery to you today?

The New Testament tells us that the church was a mystery hidden in God. Ephesians 3:9 says, "To enlighten all that they may see what the economy of the mystery is, which throughout the ages has been hidden in God, who created all things." From the beginning of the world the purpose of creation was hidden in God as a mystery. All creatures could see that there is a creation, but no one knew what the purpose of it is. (*Basic Principles for the Practice of the Church Life*, pp. 8-9)

First let us see what a mystery is. According to common understanding, a mystery is something hidden and generally unknown to people. The meaning of the mystery mentioned in the Bible, however, goes beyond this. Strictly speaking, in the Bible a mystery not only refers to things that are incomprehensible and unknown to men but also to things that are hidden in God's heart.

For example, the universe with all the things created by God is very evident and therefore not a mystery. However, the purpose of God's creation of the universe is a mystery. All the people in the world have seen the God-created universe, but from the ancient days to the present time, very few have been able to fathom the purpose of God's creation. This is because the purpose for the creation of the universe was hidden in God's heart. It is nearly impossible for man to touch God's purpose, God's plan, which is hidden in His heart. Hence, it is a mystery. This is the principle concerning mysteries mentioned in the Bible. (*Our Vision—Christ and the Church*, pp. 29-30)

Further Reading: CWWL, 1965, vol. 1, "The Vision, Practice, and Building Up of the Church as the Body of Christ," chs. 1-3; *The Conclusion of the New Testament*, msg. 190

Enlightenment and inspiration: _____

_____

_____

_____

Morning Nourishment

Eph. That by revelation the mystery was made known
3:3-5 to me, as I have written previously in brief, by
which, in reading *it,* you can perceive my understanding in the mystery of Christ, which in other
generations was not made known to the sons of
men, as it has now been revealed to His holy apostles and prophets in spirit.

In Ephesians 3:9 Paul speaks of "the economy of the mystery…, which throughout the ages has been hidden in God, who
created all things." God's mystery is His hidden purpose. His
purpose is to dispense Himself into His chosen people. Hence,
there is the economy of the mystery of God. This mystery was
hidden in God from the ages (that is, from eternity) and
through all past ages, but now it has been brought to light to
the New Testament believers.

God's intention in His creation of all things, including man,
was that man would be mingled with God to produce the church.
Zechariah 12:1 says that the Lord stretched forth the heavens,
laid the foundations of the earth, and formed the spirit of man
within him. This indicates that the heavens are for the earth,
that the earth is for man, and that man with the human spirit
is for God. God's marvelous creation, focused on man, is for the
purpose of producing the church. Therefore, Ephesians 3:9
speaks of the mystery hidden in God, who created all things.
(*The Conclusion of the New Testament,* p. 2055)

Today's Reading

Job complained that God, knowing that he was not wicked
and not acquitting him of his iniquity, ill-treated him without
cause on his side and attacked him again and again according to
what was hidden in God's heart (Job 10:1-17). Job said to God,
"Make known to me why You contend with me" (v. 2b). In verse 13
he went on to say, "You have hidden these things in Your heart; / I
know that this is with You." This indicates that Job could not find
the reason for God's treatment of him, but he believed that there

had to be some reason hidden in God's heart. Job was right; something was hidden in God's heart. Ephesians 3:9 tells us of the mystery hidden in God. This is the mystery of the ages.

Adam himself did not know why God created him in His image according to His likeness (Gen. 1:26). God kept His intention hidden throughout the ages, not telling Enoch, Noah, Abraham, Moses, David, Solomon, Isaiah, or any of the prophets. The Creator did a lot in His creation, but before the New Testament time He did not unveil to anyone what His purpose was.

The hidden mystery is that God in His Divine Trinity desires to be dispensed and wrought into His creation, man, to make man His duplication, to make man His expression. (*Life-study of Job,* pp. 50-51)

One day the Lord came, and He died, resurrected, ascended, came down as the Holy Spirit, and raised up a number of persons. Some of these persons were apostles, prophets, and teachers, who received the revelation. The mystery hidden in God was revealed to them at that time. They saw and came to know that the purpose of creation is to have the church. The church was a mystery hidden in God in the past generations until it was revealed to the apostles and prophets in the New Testament time. (*Basic Principles for the Practice of the Church Life,* pp. 9-10)

The Bible, which consists of sixty-six books, begins with God and His creation in Genesis and consummates with the New Jerusalem in Revelation. Between these two ends of the Bible, there are history, teachings, prophecies, and types. But if we understand the Bible only according to these things, we still do not know the Bible. We need to see the eternal economy of God, which is God's eternal intention with His heart's desire to dispense Himself in His Divine Trinity as the Father in the Son by the Spirit into His chosen people to be their life and nature that they may be the same as He is for His fullness, His expression. (*Life-study of Job,* p. 57)

Further Reading: The Conclusion of the New Testament, msg. 337; *Life-study of Ephesians,* msg. 29

Enlightenment and inspiration: _____

_____

_____

_____

Morning Nourishment

Eph. To me, less than the least of all saints, was this
3:8-9 grace given to announce to the Gentiles the unsearchable riches of Christ as the gospel and to
enlighten all *that they may see* what the economy
of the mystery is, which throughout the ages has
been hidden in God, who created all things.

According to Ephesians 3:4 the church has a particular title—
the mystery of Christ. God is a mystery. He is real, living, and
almighty, but invisible. No one has ever seen God (John 1:18a),
and therefore God is a mystery. This mysterious God is embodied in Christ; hence, Christ is the mystery of God (Col. 2:2). In
Ephesians 3:4 Paul used the expression *the mystery of Christ* to
explain the church as the Body of Christ in God's eternal economy, indicating that the church is the mystery of Christ. (*Truth
Lessons—Level Four,* vol. 1, p. 136)

Today's Reading

The first thing which God may have done before the foundation of the world in eternity past was to make an economy to
produce the church to manifest God. The economy of the mystery hidden in God throughout the ages was to produce the
church for the showing forth of God's multifarious wisdom.
(*The History of God in His Union with Man,* p. 17)

We must also have the high standard of the gospel concerning
the economy of the mystery hidden in God (Eph. 3:9-11)....This
deeper mystery is the purpose, the meaning, and the significance
of the universe. This mystery was not known to man but was
revealed to the apostles, especially to the apostle Paul. Thus, Paul
told us that he preached not only the unsearchable riches of
Christ but also the economy of this mystery hidden in God from
the ages....What God desires is to gain a group of people to contain
Him that they may become the members of the Body of Christ,
that Christ may be their life, their Head, and their manifestation,
and that they and He could be one universal new man to express
Christ as the embodied God to fulfill His eternal purpose. The

mystery of God is Christ, the mystery of Christ is the church, and Christ and the church are the great mystery (5:32) hidden in God from the centuries and revealed to the apostle Paul.

The highest gospel is the gospel of Christ with the church. We must value, appreciate, and treasure the church. We enjoy the church life as the highest standard of the gospel.

The gospel concerning the economy of the mystery hidden in God is to produce the church for God's expression and glorification according to God's eternal plan, or purpose. The church is so lovable because it is the very expression and glorification of God. When God has the church, He is expressed and He is glorified. We need to enjoy God in His expression and in His glorification in such a high standard.

Paul preached the divine economy as the very gospel. Ephesians 3:8 reveals the gospel of the unsearchable riches of Christ, while verse 9 reveals the gospel of the economy of the mystery hidden in God throughout the ages. We must realize, experience, and preach this economy to the new ones as the high standard of the gospel. Many Christians enjoy the gospel of grace, and some enjoy the gospel in the aspect of life, but few among today's Christians enjoy the gospel of the kingdom by being under the divine ruling in the divine life. Few enjoy the gospel of the unsearchable riches of Christ and the gospel of the economy of the mystery hidden in God from the ages. (*CWWL, 1987,* vol. 2, "The God-ordained Way to Practice the New Testament Economy," pp. 415-417, 416)

The regenerated ones, who are divinely human and humanly divine, spontaneously become an organism, the Body of Christ, which is the church of God as the new man in God's new creation to carry out God's new "career," that is, to build up the Body of Christ for the fullness, the expression, of the Triune God. This fullness as the organism of the Triune God will consummate in the New Jerusalem. (*Life-study of Job,* p. 58)

Further Reading: The God-ordained Way to Practice the New Testament Economy, ch. 26; *Truth Lessons—Level Four,* vol. 1, lsn. 13

Enlightenment and inspiration: _____

_____

_____

_____

Hymns, #1229

1 The church is Christ's deep longing
   And His good pleasure too.
   His every word and action
   Is made with her in view.
   His heart's love is established,
   And naught can Him deter;
   Before the earth's foundation
   His thoughts were filled with her.

2 The eve of all creation
   He mused on His delight,
   And pondered every feature,
   Well-pleasing in His sight.
   Creation sprang to being,
   But deep in Him did hide
   A heart of depth unfathomed
   Fixed on a glorious Bride.

3 And thus His will was 'stablished
   His counterpart to gain:
   This blessed, firm intention,
   Eternally the same.
   Though sin should e'en beguile man,
   Then mock his helpless state,
   He never could forsake her,
   His yearning ne'er abate.

4 Then mercy richly flourished,
   And love was, oh, so vast,
   As graciously He sought her
   With wisdom unsurpassed.
   The love He gave to win her
   God only comprehends!
   His life laid down, an offering
   Whose fragrance yet ascends.

5 And now in resurrection
   To her He draws most near,
   And with untold affection
   In glory does appear.
   As she beholds her Bridegroom,
   His glory floods her heart,
   'Til she, His Bride, is raptured,
   His longed-for counterpart.

*Composition for prophecy with main point and
sub-points:* _____

_____

_____

_____

_____

_____

_____

_____

_____

_____

_____

_____

_____

_____

_____

_____

_____

_____

_____

_____

_____

_____

_____

_____

_____

_____

_____

_____

_____

_____

_____

_____

_____

_____

The Original Condition of the Church,
the Degradation of the Church,
and the Recovery of the Church

Scripture Reading: Matt. 16:18; Rev. 1:11; Acts 14:23; Titus
1:5; Col. 1:18; 2:19

Day 1   I. **Our history in the Lord's recovery is not**
that of an organization or of a movement; it
is a history of recovery (John 1:1; 1 John 1:1):
   A. In Matthew 19:8 we see the principle of recovery: "From the beginning it has not been so":
      1. Recovery means to go back to the beginning;
      we need to go back to the beginning, receiv-
      ing the Lord's grace to go back to God's orig-
      inal intention, to what God ordained in the
      beginning.
      2. The word *recovery* means that something was
      there originally and then was degraded, dam-
      aged, or lost; thus, there is a need to bring that
      thing back to its original state and to its nor-
      mal condition (Dan. 1:1-2; Ezra 1:5; 6:5).
   B. When we speak of the recovery of the church, we
   mean that the church was there originally, that
   it became degraded, and that there is the need
   to bring the church back to its original state.
   C. The Lord's recovery of the church brings us back
   to the beginning for the fulfillment of God's eternal purpose and original intention regarding the
   church (Eph. 1:4-5, 22-23; 3:9-11).
   II. **We need to understand the recovery of the**
   church in relation to God's intention and ac-
   complishment and Satan's work of destruc-
   tion (v. 11):
   A. The New Testament reveals that regarding the
   church, God has a definite intention, purpose,
   and goal; first, God purposed, and then He came
   in to accomplish His purpose (Rev. 4:11; Eph.
   1:4-5, 9, 11, 22-23).

B. The New Testament also gives us a clear record
of how God's enemy came in to destroy what God
had accomplished (Matt. 16:18; 13:24-32):
  1. The satanic way to destroy God's accomplish-
     ment has an inward aspect and an outward
     aspect:
     a. The inward aspect is to damage and cor-
        rupt God's people (Acts 5:3).
     b. The outward aspect is to destroy God's
        accomplishment (Matt. 13:32).
  2. Satan produced many substitutes for Christ,
     divided the Body of Christ, and killed the
     function of the members of the Body by the
     clergy-laity system (Col. 2:8; Rev. 2:6, 14-15).
C. Because God is a purposeful God with an eternal purpose and because once He has determined
to do something, nothing can change His mind
or stop Him; after Satan's destruction God comes
in to redo the things that He had done before
(Ezra 1:3-11; 6:3-5).
D. God's redoing of what He has accomplished is
His recovery; this is to bring back whatever has
been lost and destroyed by Satan and to recover
the church according to His eternal purpose and
original intention (Matt. 19:8; 16:18).

Day 2 **III. In order to recognize the need for the recovery
of the church, we need to know the original
condition of the church and the degradation
of the church:**
A. The original condition of the church had the following characteristics:
  1. In the original church there was no hierar-
     chy among the believers (Rom. 12:4-5):
     a. The believers were all brothers without
        distinction in rank (Matt. 23:8).
     b. As members of the Body, the believers co-
        ordinated with one another on an equal
        level, and each one fulfilled his particu-
        lar function (Rom. 12:4-5).

c. The believers were all priests to God, without an intermediary class or the distinctions between clergy and laity (1 Pet. 2:5, 9).

2. The early church was completely separated from the world; it was in the world but not of the world (Rom. 12:2; 1 John 2:15; 2 Cor. 6:14-17).

3. The original church forsook idols and fully allowed God to speak (1 John 5:21).

Day 3
4. There was only one church, one expression of the Body of Christ, in a locality (1 Cor. 12:27; 1:2; Rev. 1:11).

5. The churches were one in fellowship, but each one was independent in administration, and there was no head church or federation (1 Cor. 10:16).

6. The churches honored Christ as the Head and allowed the Holy Spirit to have authority (Col. 1:18; 2:19; Acts 13:1-2; 10:19-20; 11:12).

B. The degradation of the church involved hierarchy, union with the world, idols, divisions, not allowing God to speak, having organization for unification, and usurping the headship of Christ and encroaching on the authority of the Holy Spirit.

Day 4
IV. **The recovery of the church has been gradual and progressive:**

A. Before the end of the first century, the Lord's recovery began, and century by century the recovery has continued on (2 Tim. 2:19-26).

B. In the sixteenth century Martin Luther rose up to begin the Reformation, and the sealed Bible was unlocked; based upon the Bible, he recovered justification by faith, but the proper church life was not recovered (Rom. 1:17):

1. The Protestant churches were not separated from the world, and they did not eliminate the intermediary class.

2. Among the Protestant churches there were
   more divisions, and the various denominations did not put away organization for unification.
3. The denominations did not allow Christ to
   have the absolute position and did not allow
   the Holy Spirit to have absolute authority.
C. In the eighteenth century Zinzendorf was raised
   up by the Lord to lead the Moravian brothers to a
   recovery of the church life; they were separated
   from the world, removed distinctions of rank,
   emphasized fellowship and coordination, endeavored to keep the oneness, removed formal organization for unification, and allowed Christ to be the
   Head and the Holy Spirit to rule among them.
D. In the nineteenth century the Lord raised up a
   group of brothers in England, who went further
   in the recovery of the church life (Rev. 3:7-13):
   1. In the hands of the Brethren, the Bible was
      truly an opened book, a shining book, for
      they absolutely obeyed the Lord's word; many
      important truths were released through them
      (1 Tim. 2:4).
   2. They absolutely eliminated hierarchy and
      were brothers together and members one of
      another with an emphasis on mutual love
      and fellowship.
   3. They eliminated sectarianism and main-
      tained the testimony of oneness.
Day 5   4. However, in certain aspects they were a fail-
      ure, and because of this the Lord could not
      go on at that time anywhere in the Western
      world.
E. We need to see the crucial points of the recovery
   of the church in the Far East:
   1. In 1933 and 1934 we clearly saw a crucial
      matter—the principle of the church taking
      a locality as its boundary (Acts 14:23; Titus
      1:5; Rev. 1:11):

      a. On the one hand, this prevents division and confusion; on the other hand, it also prevents "extra-local" unions.

      b. According to the teaching of the Bible, the church in each locality should live directly before the Lord and be responsible to the Head, Christ (Col. 1:18; 2:19; Acts 13:1-2).

2. We kept the principle of the administration of the church being local and the fellowship of the church being universal (14:23; 2:42; 1 Cor. 10:16-17):

      a. The church in each locality has its own administration, and the administration of the church cannot go beyond the local boundary.

      b. The fellowship of the church should not only be local; rather, it should be universal because it is the fellowship of the Body of Christ.

3. We clearly saw that churches in different localities should not have an organization for unification, for all churches should be directly under the ruling of Christ, the Head, and should directly obey the authority of the Holy Spirit (Col. 1:18; Acts 13:1-2).

4. We emphasized the universal priesthood; that is, we stressed the fact that every believer is a priest (1 Pet. 2:5, 9).

5. We also emphasized the Body's coordination in service, exhorting all the saints to keep the principle of the Body by serving together in coordination (Rom. 12:4-5; 1 Cor. 12:12-27).

6. We emphasized the practical service in the church (Rom. 12:5-11).

Day 6   V. **The Lord's recovery is different from today's Christianity; it is impossible for there to be reconciliation between the recovery and Christianity (Matt. 13:31-33, 44-46; Rev. 18:4; 19:1-3, 7-9):**

A. The recovery of the church is for bringing us out of the unscriptural system of clergy-laity back to the beginning for the pure practice of the church life according to the divine revelation (2:6, 15; Matt. 16:18; Eph. 2:20-22).

B. The history among us has been one of coming completely out of Christianity without compromise (Ezra 1:3-11; 6:3-5; Rev. 18:4).

C. There should be no bridge between the local churches and Christianity; we should be what we are without compromise or pretense, maintaining the gap between us and Christianity (1:11; Gal. 1:4).

Morning Nourishment

Eph. In order that now to the rulers and the authorities
3:10-11 in the heavenlies the multifarious wisdom of God
might be made known through the church, according to the eternal purpose which He made in
Christ Jesus our Lord.

We have to realize that our history is not that of an organization or of a movement. It is a history of the Lord's recovery....
The Lord's recovery brings us back to the beginning to have the
proper church life. In the early days of the Lord's recovery in
China, the Lord showed us the wrongdoings of Christendom,
on the negative side, and the church, on the positive side. (*CWWL,
1973-1974,* vol. 1, "The History of the Church and the Local
Churches," p. 109)

Today's Reading

[In Matthew 19:8], instead of arguing with the Pharisees,
the Lord said, "Moses, because of your hardness of heart,
allowed you to divorce your wives, but from the beginning it
has not been so." The commandment concerning divorce given
by Moses was a deviation from God's original ordination, but
Christ as the heavenly King recovered it back to the beginning
for the kingdom of the heavens.

In verse 8 we see the principle of recovery. Recovery means to
go back to the beginning. Things that exist may not date back to
the beginning.... In the beginning, God ordained one husband and
one wife, and there was no divorce. Because of the hardness of the
people's hearts, Moses tolerated divorce and allowed a man to
divorce his wife by giving her a writing of divorce. The Lord was
asking the Pharisees if they would care for God's ordination or for
the hardness of their heart. Every seeker of God should say, "O
Lord, have mercy upon me that I may care for Your original ordination. I do not want to care for the hardness of my heart. I con-
demn and reject the hardness of my heart and return to Your
original ordination." This is what is meant by recovery.

Today many Christians are arguing for certain things. Because of the hardness of the fallen human heart, the Lord tolerates some of those things. Should we agree with this toleration and the hardness of the human heart? Certainly not. Rather, we must receive the Lord's grace to go back to God's original ordination. We must go back to the beginning. (*Life-study of Matthew*, pp. 627-628)

The word *recover* means to obtain again something that has been lost, or to return something to a normal condition. *Recovery* means the restoration or return to a normal condition after a damage or a loss has been incurred....Because the church has become degraded through the many centuries of its history, it needs to be restored according to God's original intention. Concerning the church, our vision should be governed not by the present situation nor by traditional practice but by God's original intention and standard as revealed in the Scriptures.

We need to understand the recovery of the church in relation to God's intention and accomplishment and Satan's work of destruction. The New Testament reveals that regarding the church God has a definite intention, purpose, and goal. The New Testament also gives us a clear picture of God's accomplishment according to His intention. First, God purposed and then He came in to accomplish His purpose. Furthermore, the New Testament also gives us a clear record of how God's enemy came in to destroy what God had accomplished. The satanic way to destroy God's accomplishment has two aspects: the inward and the outward. The inward aspect is to damage and corrupt God's people. Then Satan seeks to destroy God's accomplishment outwardly. Nevertheless, God is a God with an eternal purpose. He is a purposeful God, and once He has made up His mind to do something, nothing can change His mind or stop Him. Therefore, after Satan's destruction, God comes in to redo the things that He had done before. This redoing is His recovery. This is to bring back whatever has been lost and destroyed by God's enemy, Satan. (*The Conclusion of the New Testament*, pp. 2447-2448)

Further Reading: The Conclusion of the New Testament, msgs. 223-224; The History of the Church and the Local Churches, ch. 1

Enlightenment and inspiration: _____

_____

_____

_____

Morning Nourishment

Matt. But you, do not be called Rabbi, for One is your
23:8 Teacher, and you are all brothers.
Rom. And do not be fashioned according to this age, but
12:2 be transformed by the renewing of the mind that
you may prove what the will of God is, that which
is good and well pleasing and perfect.

After Satan began by using so many substitutes to usurp the
place of Christ, he invented the clergy-laity system....Originally, all
the members without exception were normal, functioning members. But gradually the enemy set up the clergy-laity system to
limit the function to just a small number of believers. Since the majority have been put out of function, the Body has been paralyzed.

His first step is to replace the life. He does this with anything
other than Christ. His second step is to kill the function. He has
done this by installing the clergy-laity system.

We must see the evil strategy of the enemy, Satan, behind
these moves....Every believer must be a functioning member in
the Body. (*Satan's Strategy against the Church,* pp. 6-7)

Today's Reading

Only after we understand the original condition of the church
can we know how the church has degraded and deviated, and only
then can we know the matters that have been recovered and corrected and...what matters still need to be recovered and corrected.

Concerning the original condition of the church,...we can
look...at some important points related to the testimony and the
ground of the church so that through them we can know the
church, including her principle, her constitution, and her ground.

One of the characteristics of the original church was that there
was no hierarchy among the saved ones. They were all members
one of another, coordinating mutually and serving together.

First, all the saved ones are brothers without any distinctions
in rank. When the Lord was on the earth, He told the disciples
clearly, "The rulers of the Gentiles lord it over them, and the great
exercise authority over them. It shall not be so among you [that is,

in the church]; but whoever wants to become great among you shall be your servant, and whoever wants to be first among you shall be your slave" (Matt. 20:25-27; 23:8-11)....All the believers are brothers on the same level; there are no distinctions involving some who are higher and some who are lower.

Second, all the believers are members of the Body of Christ; as such, they coordinate with each other on an equal level, and each of them fulfills his particular function. This is shown very clearly in Romans 12:4-5, 1 Corinthians 12:12-27, and Ephesians 4:16. Without exception, every saved one is a member of the Body of Christ....As long as a person is saved, he is a member with a particular function in the church and should serve the Lord in coordination with all the saints.

Third, all the believers are priests to God. In the Old Testament, among the people of Israel there was a group who served as priests, and the rest of the Israelites were common people....But in the New Testament, in the church, there is no longer such an intermediary class; rather, all the believers are priests to God, without any distinctions between the so-called clergy and laity. The normal condition is for all the people of God to be priests to Him.

Another marked feature of the early church was that it was completely separated from the world; it was in the world but not of the world, just as the Lord said in John 17:14-17 and 18:36.

Whereas idols are adversaries of God, the church is the testimony of God. If the church has idols, the nature of the church has been changed. This is a certain fact. From Acts 15:29 we can see that the original church forsook idols in a very thorough way.

In the original church there was no human opinion and no human system; instead, the believers completely allowed the Spirit to speak through the Scriptures. They allowed the Holy Scriptures of God to have their position, and they also allowed the Holy Spirit of God to have His position. (*The Testimony and the Ground of the Church,* pp. 187, 191-193, 195)

Further Reading: The Conclusion of the New Testament, msgs. 225, 231

Enlightenment and inspiration: _____

_____

_____

_____

Morning Nourishment

Acts
13:1-2

Now there were in Antioch, in the local church, prophets and teachers....And as they were ministering to the Lord and fasting, the Holy Spirit said, Set apart for Me now Barnabas and Saul for the work to which I have called them.

The original church also had another notable feature; there was only one expression in each locality....It was one in Jerusalem (Acts 8:1), one in Antioch (13:1), one in Ephesus (Rev. 2:1), and one in Corinth (1 Cor. 1:2)....Originally, one locality had only one group of Christians, one church. This principle is very strict; that is, in one locality there should be only one church. (*The Testimony and the Ground of the Church*, pp. 195-196)

Today's Reading

Originally, although the fellowship among the churches was one, they were independent of each other in administration; there was no head church or any federation among them. In principle, a local church should live directly before Christ and honor Christ as the Head....This situation prevents division, retains the headship of Christ, and allows the Holy Spirit to have the authority.

The church is the Body of Christ, and Christ is the Head of the church (Col. 1:18; Eph. 4:15), reigning in the church through the Holy Spirit (Acts 13:2; 15:28). It was this way in the early church. There was neither human opinion nor human authority. The believers...honored Christ as the Head and obeyed the authority of the Holy Spirit; this was the supreme characteristic of the original church.

Regrettably, this kind of situation did not last long; after a short time, the church gradually became degraded and lost its original condition.

The first item of the degradation of the church is having hierarchy. This occurred as early as the beginning of the second century. At that time there was an elder in the church in Rome whose name was Clement. In his epistle he clearly referred to the matter of bringing the Judaic priestly system into the church.

The second item of the degradation of the church is being in union with the world. In A.D. 313 the Roman Emperor Constantine accepted the Christian religion, thereby bringing the church into union with the Roman Empire, that is, with the world.

The third item is the bringing in of idols. This is an even more serious matter. In its degradation, the church was filled with all kinds of idols; this can be seen in the Roman Catholic Church.

The fourth item in the degradation of the church is not letting God speak. At a certain time the Church of Rome locked up the Holy Bible and took the pope's words as their criteria. Thus, they did not allow God to speak; they shut the mouth of God.

In the degradation of the church the fifth item is having divisions. From the second century or at the latest the beginning of the third century, a small number of the people in the church began to separate themselves from the majority due to differences in the interpretation of the truth and differences in systems.

The sixth item in the degradation of the church is having organization for unification. This damaged the principle of the original church of "one city, one church." As early as the middle part of the third century, Cyprian had suggested unifying the churches. He also used the term *catholic church,* meaning "universal church."

The most serious point of the degradation of the church is the usurpation of the headship of Christ and the encroachment upon the authority of the Holy Spirit. When the church began to have an unlawful organization for unification, Christ lost His position in the church and the Holy Spirit could no longer rule in the church.... [Today] all of the characteristics of the church have become completely degraded; none of its original characteristics are left. From the inside to the outside, from the principle to the nature, from the inner reality to the outward appearance, from the testimony to the ground, everything of the church has become degraded. (*The Testimony and the Ground of the Church,* pp. 199-201, 203-207)

Further Reading: The Testimony and the Ground of the Church, Section Three, chs. 1-2

Enlightenment and inspiration: _____

_____
_____
_____

Morning Nourishment

Rev.   I know your works; behold, I have put before you an
3:8   opened door which no one can shut, because you
       have a little power and have kept My word and
       have not denied My name.

1 Tim. ...Our Savior God, who desires all men to be saved
2:3-4   and to come to the full knowledge of the truth.

We see that before the end of the first century, the Lord's recovery began. Thereafter, history shows us that, century by century, the recovery continued on. At times it was dim, but it was gradually becoming stronger and stronger. This went on until the 1500s, when Brother Martin Luther was raised up in Germany. He inherited the items of recovery from the past and culminated all the Lord's recoveries during the preceding sixteen centuries. But this does not mean that the recovery was completed; rather, it continued on. (*The New Testament Priests of the Gospel*, p. 103)

Today's Reading

By the sixteenth century,...the sealed Bible was unlocked. This was a great accomplishment of Luther. Based on the Bible, he also recovered the truth of justification by faith. However, the ways of serving in the church and preaching the gospel remained unchanged. (*The New Testament Priests of the Gospel*, p. 29)

The beginning of the Protestant church was the formation of various state churches; thus, the church fell into the hands of political governments. Therefore, the Protestant church was not freed from the world; it was still, in principle, the same as the Roman Catholic Church which was mixed with the Roman Empire.

The Protestant church did not eliminate the intermediary class.

When the Protestant church began, there was a division into numerous state churches according to distinctions of nations and national boundaries. Later, due to the promotion of different truths, the adoption of different policies and systems, and the holding of different spiritual giants in high respect, the church was further divided into many private churches.

The various denominations of the Protestant church also

established respective headquarters for unification.

In summary, although the Protestant church was much improved in comparison to the Roman Catholic Church, it did not have a thorough recovery—it did not allow Christ to have the absolute position or the Holy Spirit to have the absolute authority.

After another two hundred years, in the early part of the eighteenth century, God had a further recovery with [Brother Zinzendorf and] the Moravian brethren.

The Moravian brethren not only had the Bible in their hands, but they also obeyed the words of the Bible....They were truly freed, separated, from the world. They did not mix themselves with politics....They were absolutely not defiled by idols....They removed distinctions in rank....They also endeavored to keep the oneness by abandoning differences in doctrinal views....In this recovery,...they did not have a head church and branch churches....In such a situation, the Moravian brethren allowed Christ to be the Head and allowed the Holy Spirit to rule among them. (*The Testimony and the Ground of the Church*, pp. 213, 215-218)

In the nineteenth century, there was a further recovery when the Brethren were raised up. (*CWWL, 1989*, vol. 2, "The New Testament Priests of the Gospel," p. 30)

This recovery was very thorough....First, they obeyed the Lord's word absolutely....Many important truths were released at that time....It was not until the time of the Brethren that the hierarchy in the church was truly and thoroughly eliminated....They were purely before God as brothers and as fellow members of the Body of Christ, paying attention especially to mutual love and fellowship.

The matter of leaving the denominations began with them.... They came together to maintain the testimony of the oneness of the church. (*The Testimony and the Ground of the Church*, pp. 219-222)

Further Reading: The Testimony and the Ground of the Church,
  Section Three, ch. 3; Three Aspects of the Church, Book Two:
  The Course of the Church, chs. 13-14

Enlightenment and inspiration: _____

_____

_____

Morning Nourishment

1 Cor. The cup of blessing which we bless, is it not the fel-
10:16-17 lowship of the blood of Christ? The bread which we
break, is it not the fellowship of the body of Christ?
Seeing that there is one bread, we who are many
are one Body; for we all partake of the one bread.

The Lord had to go on in His recovery. In the nineteenth century, the Lord raised up a group of brothers in Great Britain.
They went further in the recovery of the church life, but in certain aspects they were still a failure. Because of this the Lord
could not go on at that time anywhere in the Western world.

In the beginning of the twentieth century the Lord came to the
Far East and raised up a young Chinese brother by the name of
Watchman Nee. Initially, the help he received was inherited from
the Brethren. But after ten years he discovered that what he had
received was not that complete. As a result, he had a turn, even
many turns. (*The New Testament Priests of the Gospel*, p. 103)

Today's Reading

In 1933 and 1934 we clearly saw a crucial matter—the principle of the church taking a locality as its boundary....In many places
there were brothers who rose up to meet together, but there was a
question concerning the boundary of each of these meetings....A
certain brother, after spending much effort in studying the Bible,
found that the church takes a locality as its ground and boundary;
that is, he saw the light of one locality, one church.

Based on this principle, from 1934 onward, no matter how large
or how small a city is, we have taken the way of having only one
church. On one hand, this prevents division and confusion; on the
other hand, it also prevents "extra-local" unions. If one locality were
united with another locality, it would cause Christ to lose His position and the Holy Spirit to lose His authority. This is not pleasing to
the Lord, and it is most offensive to the Lord. According to the
teaching of the Bible, the church in each locality should live directly
before the Lord and be responsible to the Head, Christ. There
should be no superior church, no head church, and no federation.

Because we saw the preceding item, we all kept one principle: the administration of the church is local, and the fellowship of the church is universal. From the Word of God we clearly saw that the church in each locality has its own administration and is independent of the other churches. Each local church has its own eldership and its own administration. The administration of the church cannot go beyond the locality; once it goes beyond the local boundary, it causes the church to lose its local nature. Thus, the churches in all the localities will not be able to live directly before Christ, the Head. The fellowship of the church should not only be local; rather, it should also be universal because it is the fellowship of the Body of Christ. A local church should have fellowship with all the other churches; otherwise, it will be a sect.

We also clearly saw that churches in different localities should not have an organization for unification, because the administration of the church is local. All churches should be directly under the ruling of Christ, the Head, and should directly obey the authority of the Holy Spirit.

In addition, we also emphasized the universal priesthood; that is, we stressed the fact that every believer is a priest. In Judaism, the majority of the people are laymen, and only a few are priests. The Roman Catholic Church and the Protestant churches adopted the Judaic system.... [But] all brothers and sisters are children of God, members of the Body of Christ, and priests to God; not only so, all can approach God and serve God directly.

We also emphasized the Body's coordination in service, exhorting all the saints to keep the principle of the Body by serving together in coordination instead of serving independently.

We also emphasized the practical church service. In all aspects of our service we did not want merely a theory; we also wanted the practice. (*The Testimony and the Ground of the Church*, pp. 232-235)

Further Reading: Three Aspects of the Church, Book 2: The Course of the Church, chs. 15-16

Enlightenment and inspiration: _____

_____

_____

_____

Morning Nourishment

Matt. Another parable He spoke to them: The kingdom
13:33 of the heavens is like leaven, which a woman took
and hid in three measures of meal until the whole
was leavened.

Rev. ...I heard another voice out of heaven, saying, Come
18:4 out of her, My people, that you do not participate in
her sins and that you do not receive her plagues.

The Lord's recovery is absolutely different from today's religion. We are not concerned with knowing the Bible merely in letters. We are here to carry out God's economy in His recovery. It is
impossible for there to be reconciliation between the recovery and
Christianity. In the recovery we repudiate the wood, the grass, and
the stubble. But these inferior materials are not only welcomed
by many Christians—they are appreciated, praised, exalted, and
advertised....In the recovery we would rather have a small amount
of gold, silver, and precious stones than a huge pile of wood, grass,
and stubble....The spiritual eyes of many religious leaders and
Bible teachers are blind. They may study the Word in letters, but
they do not know the mysterious reality of verses such as Exodus
25:1-9. We do not care for the traditional teachings but for God's
revelation in His Word. (*Life-study of Exodus,* pp. 967-968)

Today's Reading

Because Christendom is a mixture, when one gets the fine
flour, he also gets the leaven because these two have become
one. This is why it has been difficult for us to fully come out of
Christendom.

Although I had contact with Brother Nee's ministry in 1925, I
did not come into the Lord's recovery in a full way until 1932. Since
that time I have seen the recovery passing through a process of
coming out of Christendom. Even today we have not come out of
Christendom in a thorough way. We still have something of Christendom within us, even unconsciously. When we come to a meeting,
we may expect a good speaker to speak to us. In nature, this is the
element and cause of fallen Christendom. This is the evil element

of Nicolaitanism, the clergy-laity system, which the Lord hates (Rev. 2:6). Why do we not come to the meetings prepared to minister something? We may say that we are weak, but we are strong in expecting to listen to a good message. We may dislike going to a meeting where there is not a good speaker. This is the subtle element of the clergy-laity system still remaining within us.

The Lord's recovery is for bringing us out of this unscriptural system and back to the beginning of the pure practice of the church life according to the divine revelation.

I am sharing this to help us realize that the history among us has been one of coming completely out of Christianity without compromise. It is a shame that some so-called co-workers among us have tried their best to compromise. They say that between the denominations and the local churches there is a gap, and they consider themselves as the bridge to bridge the gap.

Because of our standing for the pure church life, others have been offended. But what can we do? Paul said in Galatians 1:10, "If I were still trying to please men, I would not be a slave of Christ." If we were men-pleasers, we would not suffer persecution as Paul did. The history of the Lord's recovery is a history of coming out of and being outside of the present evil age. We have burned the bridges between us and Christianity, but some among us have tried to build a bridge to bring us back. We need to burn all the bridges. There should be no bridge between the local churches and Christianity. Everything should be after its kind. The denominations are after their kind, and the local churches should be after their kind. We should be what we are without compromise or pretense.

We need to maintain such a gap between us and Christianity. The wider this gap is the better because it is a gap between us and the present evil age....Our history is a history outside of the present evil age. (*CWWL, 1973-1974,* vol. 1, "The History of the Church and the Local Churches," pp. 110, 94-96)

Further Reading: CWWL, 1973-1974, vol. 1, "The History of the Church and the Local Churches," chs. 1, 4-5, 9-10

Enlightenment and inspiration: _____

_____

_____

_____

Hymns, #1274

1 In Revelation two and three,
   The seven local churches see:
   The lessons there for you and me
   Are for the Lord's recovery.

2 The words to them are words to us,
   So that the church be glorious,
   And all their warnings we must heed
   So that the Lord can meet His need.

3 To Ephesus, the word is clear:
   "To your first love you're not so near;
   You've left to work so far away;
   Repent, return to Him today."

4 Thus, we must all turn back to Him,
   Leave other loves, for these are sin.
   Oh, let us hearken to His call—
   If we miss this, we've missed it all!

7 From Pergamos we clearly see
   The world has wed Christianity!
   And faithful Antipas did fall—
   He dared to stand against it all.

8 To wed the world we all must fear:
   His spoken word will save us here—
   If to His speaking we give heed,
   We'll separated be indeed.

9 Then Thyatira comes at length:
   Her mixture with the world her strength.
   Fine flour leavened by the yeast,
   A harlot riding on a beast.

10 Lord, we are mixed but hardly know;
    To us this mixture fully show.
    Each added thing we will refute
    Until we're wholly absolute.

12 Lord, take us all the way to life
    To overcome the deadness rife.
    Away from deadness we would flee
    That full of life we'll always be.

13 Now Philadelphia comes at last;
    That which she has she should hold fast—
    The brothers' love, the name, the word;
    This church has satisfied the Lord.

14 We as the brothers all are one;
    We're one by life, and life alone.
    If we His word and name do keep
    A glorious building God will reap.

17 Lord, shine Your light on us today
    That we may fully go Your way;
    Anoint our eyes and let us see
    So You can have recovery.

Composition for prophecy with main point and sub-points: _____

_____

_____

_____

_____

_____

_____

_____

_____

_____

_____

_____

_____

_____

_____

_____

_____

_____

The Degradation of the Church—
the Principle of Babylon
and the Way to Overcome It

Scripture Reading: Rev. 17:1-6; 18:4, 7; Lev. 1:3-4, 9; 6:10-13

Day 1   I. **The principle of Babylon (Heb. *Babel*) is man's endeavor to build up something from earth to heaven by human ability, by bricks (Gen. 11:1-9):**
          A. Stone is made by God, whereas bricks are made by man, being a human invention, a human product.
          B. Those who live according to the principle of Babylon do not see that they are limited; rather, they attempt to do the Lord's work by their natural ability with their human effort (cf. 1 Cor. 15:10, 58).
          C. The building of God is not built with man-made bricks and by human labor; it is built with God-created and transformed stones and by the divine work (3:12).
         II. **The principle of Babylon is hypocrisy (Rev. 17:4, 6; Matt. 23:25-32; Luke 12:1):**
          A. The significance of Achan's sin was his coveting a beautiful Babylonian garment in his seeking to improve himself, to make himself look better, for the sake of appearance (Josh. 7:21).
          B. This was the sin of Ananias and Sapphira, who lied to the Holy Spirit (Acts 5:1-11):
             1. They did not love the Lord very much, but they wanted to be looked upon as those who greatly loved the Lord; they were just pretending.
             2. They were not willing to offer everything cheerfully to God, but before man they acted as if they had offered all.
          C. Whenever we put on a garment that does not match our actual condition, we are in the principle of Babylon (Matt. 6:1-6; 15:7-8).

D. Everything done in falsehood to receive glory from man is done in the principle of the harlot, not in the principle of the bride (John 5:41, 44; 7:18; 12:42-43; 2 Cor. 4:5; 1 Thes. 2:4-6).

Day 2 III. **The principle of Babylon is that of not considering herself a widow but of glorifying herself and living luxuriously (Rev. 18:7):**

A. Only those believers who have fallen would consider themselves not to be a widow; in a sense, the believers in Christ are a widow in the present age because their Husband, Christ, is absent from them; because our Beloved is not here in the world, our heart is not here (Matt. 9:14-15; Luke 18:3).

B. Anything in our living that is in excess is luxury and is in the principle of Babylon (1 Tim. 6:6-10).

IV. **The principle of Babylon is the principle of a harlot (Rev. 17:1-6):**

Day 3 A. Babylon's purpose is for man to make a name for himself and deny God's name (Gen. 11:4):

1. To denominate the church by taking any name other than our Lord's is spiritual fornication (cf. Rev. 3:8).

2. The church, as the pure virgin espoused to Christ, should have no name other than her Husband's (2 Cor. 11:2; 1 Cor. 1:10).

B. Babylon means confusion (Gen. 11:6-7):

1. In the church we should not have different kinds of speaking; we should have only one mind and one mouth under one ministry with one unique teaching for the one Body (Rom. 15:5-6; 1 Cor. 1:10; Phil. 2:2; 1 Tim. 1:3-4).

2. When we are in our mind, we are in the principle of Babylon; when we are in our spirit, we are in today's Jerusalem, in which there is the divine oneness (John 4:23-24; Eph. 4:3).

3. We should not dare to have any division, because our Husband is one, and we His wife are also one (Matt. 19:3-9).

C. With the rebellious people at Babel, there was a scattering (Gen. 11:8):
   1. In the ancient time all the Israelites came together three times a year at Jerusalem; this was versus the scattering at Babel (Deut. 12:5; 16:16):
      a. It was by this unique place of worship to God, Jerusalem, that the oneness of His people was kept for generations (Psa. 133).
      b. Jerusalem not only signifies our spirit but also signifies the genuine ground of oneness, the ground of locality (Acts 8:1; 13:1; Rev. 1:11).
      c. In order to come out of Babylon, we must be "in spirit, on the ground."
   2. The sin of Jeroboam, who set up another center of worship, is the sin of division caused by one's ambition to have a kingdom, an empire, to satisfy his selfish desire (1 Kings 12:26-33).
D. Babylon is a mixture of the things of God with the things of the idols:
   1. King Nebuchadnezzar of Babylon burned the house of God in Jerusalem, carried away all the vessels that were in God's house for God's worship, and put them in the temple of his idols in Babylon (2 Chron. 36:6-7; Ezra 1:11).
   2. In the New Testament this mixture is enlarged with the great Babylon (Rev. 17:3-5; cf. 21:18; 22:1).

Day 4 V. **The Lord's call in the book of Revelation is for His people to come out of Babylon, the apostate church, so that they may return to the orthodoxy of the church (18:4-5):**
A. According to God's Word, His children cannot partake of anything that has the character of Babylon (2 Cor. 6:17-18).

B. God hates the principle of Babylon more than anything else (Rev. 17:5-6; 18:4-5; 19:2).

C. Anything that is halfway and not absolute is called Babylon:

1. We need God to enlighten us so that in His light we may judge everything in us that is not absolute toward Him (3:16-19).

2. Only when we judge ourselves in this way can we confess that we too hate the principle of Babylon (cf. 2:6).

3. By His grace, may the Lord not allow us to seek any glory and honor outside of Christ (John 7:18; 12:26; Phil. 1:19-21a; cf. Exo. 28:2).

4. The Lord requires that we delight and seek to be one who is absolute, not one who is living in the principle of Babylon.

D. When God judges the harlot and shatters all her work, and when He casts out all that she is and the principle she represents, voices from heaven will say, "Hallelujah!" (Rev. 19:1-4).

Day 5 **VI. In order to overcome the principle of Babylon, we need to daily take Christ as our burnt offering, which typifies Christ in His living a life that is perfect and absolutely for God and for God's satisfaction and in His being the life that enables God's people to have such a living (Lev. 1:3, 9; John 5:19, 30; 6:38; 7:18; 8:29; 14:24; 2 Cor. 5:14-15; Gal. 2:19-20; Phil. 1:19-21a):**

A. By laying our hands on Christ as our burnt offering, we are joined to Him, and He and we become one; in such a union all our weaknesses, defects, and faults are taken on by Him, and all His virtues become ours; this requires us to exercise our spirit through the proper prayer so that we may be one with Him in an experiential way (Lev. 1:4).

B. When we lay our hands on Christ through prayer, the life-giving Spirit, who is the very Christ on whom we lay our hands (1 Cor. 15:45b; 2 Cor. 3:6, 17; 4:5), will immediately move and work within us to live a life that is a repetition of the life that Christ lived on earth, the life of the burnt offering (cf. Exo. 38:1).

Day 6

C. The burnt offering being kept on the hearth of the altar until the morning signifies that a burnt offering should remain in the place of burning through the dark night of this age until the morning, until the Lord Jesus comes again (Lev. 6:9; 2 Pet. 1:19).

D. The ashes, the result of the burnt offering, are a sign of God's acceptance of the offering (Lev. 6:10); the priest's putting on linen garments signifies that fineness, purity, and cleanness are needed in handling the ashes; his putting on other garments to carry the ashes outside the camp (v. 11) signifies that the handling of the ashes of the burnt offering was done in a stately manner.

E. Ashes indicate the result of Christ's death, which brings us to an end, that is, to ashes (Gal. 2:20a); the putting of the ashes beside the altar toward the east (Lev. 1:16), the side of the sunrise, is an allusion to resurrection; in relation to the burnt offering, the ashes are not the end, for Christ's death brings in resurrection (Rom. 6:3-5).

F. God has a high regard for these ashes, for eventually the ashes will become the New Jerusalem; our being reduced to ashes brings us into the transformation of the Triune God (12:2; 2 Cor. 3:18); in resurrection we as ashes are transformed to become precious materials—gold, pearl, and precious stones—for the building of the New Jerusalem.

G. "The fire on the altar shall be kept burning on it; it must not go out. And the priest shall burn wood on it every morning, and he shall lay the burnt offering in order upon it and shall burn the fat of the peace offerings on it. Fire shall be

kept burning on the altar continually; it shall
not go out" (Lev. 6:12-13):

1. The priest's burning wood on the altar every
   morning signifies the need of the serving
   one's cooperation with God's desire by adding more fuel to the holy fire to strengthen
   the burning for the receiving of the burnt
   offering as God's food; the morning signifies a new start for the burning (vv. 12-13;
   cf. Luke 12:49-50; Rom. 12:11; 2 Tim. 1:6-7).

2. The burning of the burnt offering laid a
   foundation for the sweetness of the peace
   offering; this indicates that our offering ourselves to God as a continual burnt offering
   (cf. Rom. 12:1) should be laid as a foundation
   for our sweet fellowship with God, signified
   by the burning of the fat of the peace offering; the burning of both the burnt offering
   and the peace offering signifies that both
   our absoluteness for God and our enjoyment
   of the Triune God are a matter of burning
   (Lev. 6:12-13).

Morning Nourishment

Gen. **And they said to one another, Come, let us make**
11:3-4 **bricks and burn *them* thoroughly. And they had**
brick for stone, and they had tar for mortar. And
they said, Come, let us build ourselves a city and a
tower whose top is in the heavens; and let us make
a name for ourselves, lest we be scattered over the
surface of the whole earth.

The name *Babylon* originates from "Babel."...The principle of
the tower of Babel involves the attempt to build up something
from earth to reach unto heaven. When men built this tower, they
used bricks. There is a basic difference between brick and stone.
Stone is made by God, and bricks are made by man. Bricks are a
human invention, a human product. The meaning of Babylon
relates to man's own efforts to build a tower to reach unto heaven.
Babylon represents man's ability....Everything consists of bricks
baked by man; everything depends upon man's action. Those who
are according to this principle do not see that they are limited;
rather, they attempt to do the Lord's work by their own natural
ability. They do not stand in a position where they are truly able to
say, "Lord, if You do not give us grace, we cannot do anything."
They think that man's ability can suffice for spiritual things.
Their intention is to establish something upon the earth that will
reach to heaven. (*CWWN,* vol. 34, "The Glorious Church," p. 101)

Today's Reading

Heaven is always above man. Though man may climb and
build and though he may not fall, he still will not be able to touch
heaven. God destroyed man's plan to build the tower of Babel in
order to show man that he is useless in spiritual matters. Man
cannot do anything.

Another incident in the Old Testament...outstandingly mani-
fests this principle. When the Israelites entered into the land of
Canaan, the first person to commit sin was Achan....[Achan]
said, "When I saw among the spoil a beautiful mantle of Shinar,...
I coveted them and took them" (Josh. 7:21). A Babylonian garment

seduced Achan to commit sin. What does this beautiful garment imply? A beautiful garment is worn for the sake of appearance. When one puts on a beautiful garment, it means that he adorns himself to improve his appearance and to add a little luster to himself. Achan's coveting of the Babylonian garment meant that he was seeking to improve himself, to make himself look better. This was Achan's sin.

The first ones to commit sin in the New Testament after the church began...were Ananias and Sapphira....They lied to the Holy Spirit. They did not love the Lord very much, but they wanted to be looked upon as those who greatly loved the Lord. They were just pretending. They were not willing to offer everything cheerfully to God. Before man, however, they acted as if they had offered all. This is the Babylonian garment.

The principle of Babylon, therefore, is hypocrisy. There is no reality, yet people act as if there is in order to obtain glory from man. Here is a real danger to God's children—pretending to be spiritual. There is a great deal of spiritual behavior which is acted out in falsehood. It is put on as a veneer. Many long prayers are counterfeit; many prayerful tones are unreal....Whenever we put on a garment which does not match our actual condition, we are in the principle of Babylon.

God's children do not know how much falsehood they have put on in order to receive glory from man. This is entirely opposite from the attitude of the bride. Everything done in falsehood is done in the principle of the harlot, not in the principle of the bride. It is a great matter for God's children to be delivered from pretending before man....If we set our sight upon man's glory and man's position in the church, we are participating in the sin of the Babylonian garment and the sin committed by Ananias and Sapphira. False consecration is sin, and false spirituality is also sin. True worship is in spirit and truthfulness. May God make us true men. (*CWWN*, vol. 34, "The Glorious Church," pp. 102-103)

Further Reading: CWWN, vol. 34, "The Glorious Church," ch. 5

Enlightenment and inspiration: _____

_____

_____

_____

Morning Nourishment

Rev. As much as she has glorified herself and lived lux-
18:7 uriously, as much torment and sorrow give to her;
for she says in her heart, I sit a queen, and I am not
a widow, and I shall by no means see sorrow.
17:5 And on her forehead there was a name written,
MYSTERY, BABYLON THE GREAT, THE MOTHER OF THE
HARLOTS AND THE ABOMINATIONS OF THE EARTH.

Another condition of Babylon is seen in Revelation 18:7....
She sits as a queen. She has lost all of her character of being a
widow. She has no feeling about the Lord Jesus being killed and
crucified on the cross. Rather, she says, "I sit a queen." She has
lost her faithfulness; she has missed her proper goal. This is the
principle of Babylon, and this is corrupted Christianity. (*CWWN*,
vol. 34, "The Glorious Church," p. 103)

In Revelation 18 Babylon typifies the fallen church....Only
fallen ones do not consider themselves as a widow....Oh, if we want
to serve the Lord faithfully in this world, we have to be a widow
with respect to the world. We have to maintain a widow's attitude
toward the world daily. Once the disciples of John came to Jesus,
saying, "Why do we and the Pharisees fast much, but Your disciples do not fast?" (Matt. 9:14). Jesus said unto them, "The sons of
the bridechamber cannot mourn as long as the bridegroom is
with them, can they? But days will come when the bridegroom
will be taken away from them, and then they will fast" (v. 15). Oh,
today He is no longer here. This is the time for us to fast. Are we
fasting with respect to the world? This earth is not our home; we
have no happiness on this earth because He is not here. (*CWWN*,
vol. 18, p. 407)

Today's Reading

Revelation 18 shows us many other things about Babylon,
especially regarding the luxuries she enjoyed. Concerning our
attitude toward the inventions of science, we can use many things
when we have a need. Just as the apostle Paul spoke of using the
world (1 Cor. 7:31), our purpose with these things is simply to use

them. However, luxurious enjoyment is another matter....We are not saying that we should not use certain things at all, but we are saying that anything in excess is luxury. Regardless of whether it is clothing, food, or housing, if it is excessive or beyond our need, it is luxury and in the principle of Babylon. God allows all that we need, but He does not permit things which are beyond our necessity. We should order our living according to the principle of need; then God will bless us. If we live according to our own lust, we are in the principle of Babylon, and God will not bless us. (*CWWN,* vol. 34, "The Glorious Church," pp. 103-104)

Eventually, Babylon is called "the great harlot" (Rev. 17:1) and "THE MOTHER OF THE HARLOTS" (v. 5)....A harlot is a woman having contact with males without a governing principle. A proper wife is one who keeps the governing principle, which is the principle of one wife for one husband.

In a sense, a number of Christians are like this....They travel from denomination to denomination. This is confusion. There is no governing principle. Confusion causes division, and division produces confusion. Division and confusion are very close sisters. They always go together. This is the character of a harlot!

We have to see that there is only one Christ. There is only one church. There is only one Head. There is only one Body! Regardless of where we are, we must be in that unique church.

According to the New Testament, there should be only one church for one city and one city with only one church (Acts 8:1; 13:1; Rev. 1:11). This is the governing principle of one wife with one husband. But the situation today is that of one woman with many men. This woman is Babylon, a harlot without a governing principle. Some people say that we are too narrow. But is it too narrow for a wife to have only one husband? We have to reject the principle of the harlot. A proper wife should always be narrow; she should have only one husband. (*CWWL, 1972,* vol. 1, "The Living and Practical Way to Enjoy Christ," pp. 212-213)

Further Reading: CWWN, vol. 18, pp. 405-410

Enlightenment and inspiration: _____

_____

_____

_____

Morning Nourishment

Rev. I know your works; behold, I have put before you
3:8 an opened door which no one can shut, because
you have a little power and have kept My word
and have not denied My name.

17:4 And the woman was clothed in purple and scarlet,
and gilded with gold and precious stone and pearls,
having in her hand a golden cup full of abominations and the unclean things of her fornication.

To denominate the church by taking any name other than
the Lord's is spiritual fornication. The church, as the pure virgin espoused to Christ (2 Cor. 11:2), should have no name other
than her Husband's. All other names are an abomination in the
eyes of God. (Rev. 3:8, footnote 3)

Today's Reading

In Genesis 11 with Babel you can see four main points. First,
man at that time was trying to do something against God by at-
tempting to make a name for himself (v. 4)....Babylon is good for
man to make a name, not for man to call on the name of the Lord.

Second, Babylon means confusion. Of course, you may say that
God came in to confuse the people there, to confound them. But you
have to realize that this confounding from God was a punishment
to man due to his trying to make a name for himself. He con-
founded them by causing them to have different languages. I speak
my language, and you speak yours. I have my opinion, you have
your thought, and we all are different; I do not understand you, nor
do you understand me. This is a punishment from God....Those at
Babel did not understand one another. This was done by God. He
exercised His judgment upon the rebellious human race.

The third point with those at Babel is that all of them were
scattered....In the local churches we have a gathering, not a scattering. The Bible reveals that God's people always gathered together in Jerusalem. In the ancient time all the Israelites came
together three times a year (Deut. 16:16)....They came together
at Jerusalem, but at Babel there was a scattering.

In today's Christianity the first point is that man is going to make a name. The second point is the misunderstanding between all the Christian groups and denominations. The third point is the scattering. Each one goes his own way and direction. Man's attempt to make a name for himself, confusion, and scattering are the significant points with Babel. All these points are still remaining with Christianity because it has become today's Babylon.

King Nebuchadnezzar of Babylon came to destroy Jerusalem. He burned the house of God in Jerusalem, carried away all the vessels in God's house for God's worship, and put them in the temple of his idols in Babylon (2 Chron. 36:6-7). What a contradiction this was. This shows that even in Babylon, there are some of the things related to God. In the temple of idols in Babylon, there are some vessels belonging to God's house. This brings us to the fourth point concerning Babylon: it is a mixture of the things of God with the things of the idols.

In the New Testament this mixture is enlarged. In spirit John saw a vision of the great Babylon (Rev. 17:3-5). Babylon is decorated, gilded, with all the things of the New Jerusalem. The New Jerusalem is built with three precious materials: gold, precious stones, and pearls (21:18-21). The great Babylon is gilded with gold, precious stones, and pearls. She gives people the appearance that she is the same as the New Jerusalem, but she is not built in a solid way with these precious things; she is only gilded with these treasures as ornaments for outward display. This is a deception intending to entice people. It is the harlot's false appearance.

The difference between apostate Christendom and the genuine church is that one is a mixture, but the other is pure. In the New Jerusalem there is no mixture. Everything is pure. Revelation 21:18 says the city is pure gold. Also, the river of water of life is bright as crystal (22:1). It is absolutely pure, without mixture. (*CWWL, 1972,* vol. 1, "The Living and Practical Way to Enjoy Christ," pp. 209-211)

Further Reading: CWWL, 1972, vol. 1, "The Living and Practical Way to Enjoy Christ," ch. 7; *Life-study of Revelation,* msgs. 51-52

Enlightenment and inspiration: _____
_____
_____
_____

Morning Nourishment

Rev. ...He cried with a strong voice, saying, Fallen, fallen
18:2 is Babylon the Great! And she has become a dwell-
     ing place of demons and a hold of every unclean
     spirit and a hold of every unclean and hateful bird.
  4 ...I heard another voice out of heaven, saying, Come
     out of her, My people, that you do not participate in
     her sins and that you do not receive her plagues.

What shall we do? The Lord's call in the book of Revelation
is for His people to come out of her (18:4). In the eyes of God,
Babylon is fallen (v. 2). The whole of Christianity today is the
great Babylon in the principle of a harlot. We must obey the
Lord's call to come out of her. (*CWWL, 1972*, vol. 1, "The Living
and Practical Way to Enjoy Christ," p. 214)

Today's Reading

"Therefore 'come out from their midst and be separated,
says the Lord, and do not touch what is unclean; and I will wel-
come you'; 'and I will be a Father to you, and you will be sons
and daughters to Me'" [2 Cor. 6:17-18]. According to God's Word,
His children cannot be involved in any matter containing the
character of Babylon. God said that we must come out from
every situation where man's power is mixed with God's power,
where man's ability is mixed with God's work, and where man's
opinion is mixed with God's Word. We cannot partake of anything that has the character of Babylon. We have to come out of
it. God's children must learn from the depths of their spirit to
separate themselves from Babylon and to judge all her actions.
If we do this, we will not be condemned together with Babylon.

Day by day Babylon is becoming larger and larger. But God
will judge her in the end. Revelation 19:1-4 says, "After these
things I heard as it were a loud voice of a great multitude in
heaven, saying, Hallelujah! The salvation and the glory and
the power are of our God. For true and righteous are His judg-
ments; for He has judged the great harlot who corrupted the
earth with her fornication, and He avenged the blood of His

slaves at her hand. And a second time they said, Hallelujah! And her smoke goes up forever and ever. And the twenty-four elders and the four living creatures fell down and worshipped God, who sits upon the throne, saying, Amen, Hallelujah!" When God judges the harlot and shatters all her work, and when He casts out all that she is and the principle she represents, voices from heaven will say, "Hallelujah!" In the New Testament, there are very few hallelujahs, and they are all expressed in this chapter because Babylon, she who adulterated the Word of Christ, has been judged.

The passage in Revelation 18:2-8 tells us the reason for Babylon's fall and judgment. The sinful deeds of Babylon are announced, and the consequences of her judgment are set forth. All who are of the same mind with God must say, Hallelujah, for God has judged Babylon. Though the actual judgment is in the future, the spiritual judgment must take place today....If God's children bring many unspiritual things into the church, how do we feel about it? Does the fact that we are all God's children and the fact that we should love one another mean that we should not say, Hallelujah, to God's judgment? We must realize that this is not a matter of love, but a matter of God's glory. The principle of Babylon is confusion and uncleanness; therefore, her name is the harlot.

God hates the principle of Babylon more than anything else. We must note in His presence how much of our being is still not absolute for Him. Anything which is halfway and not absolute is called Babylon. We need God to enlighten us so that in His light we may judge everything in us which is not absolute toward Him. Only when we judge ourselves in this way can we confess that we too hate the principle of Babylon. By His grace, may the Lord not allow us to seek any glory and honor outside of Christ. The Lord requires that we delight and seek to be one who is absolute, not one who is living in the principle of Babylon. (*CWWN,* vol. 34, "The Glorious Church," pp. 104-106)

Further Reading: CWWN, vol. 34, "The Glorious Church," ch. 5

Enlightenment and inspiration: _____

_____

_____

Morning Nourishment

Lev. If his offering is a burnt offering from the herd, he
1:3-4 shall present it, a male without blemish; he shall
present it at the entrance of the Tent of Meeting, that
he may be accepted before Jehovah. And he shall lay
his hand on the head of the burnt offering, and it
shall be accepted for him, to make expiation for him.

The Hebrew word [for *burnt offering* (Lev. 1:3)] literally means
that which goes up and denotes something that ascends to God.
The burnt offering typifies Christ not mainly in His redeeming
man from sin but in His living a life that is perfect and absolutely
for God and for God's satisfaction (v. 9; John 5:19, 30; 6:38; 7:18;
8:29; 14:24) and in His being the life that enables God's people to
have such a living (2 Cor. 5:15; Gal. 2:19-20). It is God's food that
God may enjoy it and be satisfied (Num. 28:2). This offering was to
be offered daily, in the morning and in the evening (Exo. 29:38-42;
Lev. 6:8-13; Num. 28:3-4). (Lev. 1:3, footnote 1)

Today's Reading

The burnt offering signifies Christ not mainly for redeeming
man's sin but for living for God and for God's satisfaction. As the
sin offering, Christ is for redeeming man's sin, but as the burnt
offering, He is absolutely for living a life which can satisfy God in
full. Throughout His life on earth, the Lord Jesus always lived a
life that satisfied God to the uttermost. In the four Gospels He is
presented as the One who is absolutely one with God. His divine
attributes were expressed in His human virtues, and sometimes
His human virtues were expressed in and with His divine attributes. When He was confronted, examined, and questioned by
the evil, subtle opposers—the scribes, the Pharisees, the Saddu-
cees, and the Herodians—during His last days on earth, at certain times His human virtues were expressed through His
divine attributes, and at other times His divine attributes were
expressed in His human virtues.

In the life of the Lord Jesus there was no blemish, defect, or
imperfection. He was perfect, and He lived a life which was per-

fect and absolutely for God. He was fully qualified to be the burnt offering. Having, through His incarnation, a body prepared for Him by God to be the real burnt offering (Heb. 10:5-6), He did God's will (vv. 7-9) and was obedient unto death (Phil. 2:8). On the cross, He offered His body to God once for all (Heb. 10:10).

The burnt offering, which was offered on the altar in the outer court, was accepted before Jehovah (Lev. 1:3). The altar signifies the cross. The cross on which Christ offered Himself was on earth, but His offering of Himself was before God. He offered Himself on earth, and He was accepted by God and before God. (*Life-study of Leviticus*, pp. 24-25, 27)

The laying on of hands signifies not substitution but identification, union (Acts 13:3 and footnote 2). By laying our hands on Christ as our offering, we are joined to Him, and He and we become one. In such a union all our weaknesses, defects, and faults are taken on by Him, and all His virtues become ours. This requires us to exercise our spirit through the proper prayer so that we may be one with Him in an experiential way (cf. 1 Cor. 6:17 and footnotes). When we lay our hands on Christ through prayer, the life-giving Spirit, who is the very Christ on whom we lay our hands (1 Cor. 15:45; 2 Cor. 3:6, 17), will immediately move and work within us to live in us a life that is a repetition of the life that Christ lived on earth, the life of the burnt offering. (Lev. 1:4, footnote 1)

The burnt offering denotes Christ's being absolute for God's satisfaction. The way to satisfy God with sweetness, peace, and rest is to live a life that is absolutely for God. Since we cannot live such a life, we must take Christ as our burnt offering. We need to lay our hands on Him to indicate that we desire to be identified with Him, one with Him, and to live the kind of life He lived on earth. Such a life includes being slaughtered, skinned, cut into pieces, and washed. By passing through all these processes, we shall have something to offer to God as our burnt offering—the very Christ whom we have experienced. (*Life-study of Leviticus*, p. 40)

Further Reading: Life-study of Leviticus, msgs. 3-4, 6

Enlightenment and inspiration: _____

_____

_____

Morning Nourishment

Lev.   ...This is the law of the burnt offering: The burnt
6:9-10 offering shall be on the hearth on the altar all night
        until the morning....And the priest shall put on his
        linen garment;...and he shall take up the ashes to
        which the fire has consumed the burnt offering on
        the altar, and he shall put them beside the altar.
12-13   ...The fire on the altar shall be kept burning on...
        the altar continually; it shall not go out.

The burnt offering being on the hearth signifies that anything offered as a burnt offering must be put on the place of
offering to be burned. Those who offer themselves to God as a
burnt offering must be on the place of burning and must be
willing to become a heap of ashes. (Lev. 6:9, footnote 2)

All night until the morning [Lev. 6:9] signifies that a burnt
offering should remain in the place of burning through the
dark night of this age until the morning, until the Lord Jesus
comes again (2 Pet. 1:19; Mal. 4:2). (Lev. 6:9, footnote 3)

Today's Reading

The ashes, the result of the burnt offering, are a sign of God's acceptance of the offering. The priest's putting on linen garments
(Lev. 6:10) signifies that fineness, purity, and cleanness are needed
in handling the ashes. His putting on other garments to carry
the ashes outside the camp (v. 11) signifies that the handling of the
ashes of the burnt offering was done in a stately manner.

Ashes indicate the result of Christ's death, which brings us to
an end, that is, to ashes (Gal. 2:20a). The putting of the ashes
beside the altar toward the east (Lev. 1:16), the side of the sunrise, is an allusion to resurrection. In relation to the burnt offering, the ashes are not the end, for Christ's death brings in resurrection (Rom. 6:3-5; 2 Cor. 4:10-12; Phil. 3:10-11). God has a high
regard for these ashes, for eventually the ashes will become the
New Jerusalem. Our being reduced to ashes brings us into the
transformation of the Triune God (Rom. 12:2; 2 Cor. 3:18). In resurrection we as ashes are transformed to become precious

materials—gold, pearl, and precious stones—for the building of the New Jerusalem (Rev. 21:18-21). (Lev. 6:10, footnote 1)

The priest's burning wood on the altar every morning signifies the need of the serving one's cooperation with God's desire (see footnote 4 on Leviticus 6:9) by adding more fuel to the holy fire to strengthen the burning for the receiving of the burnt offering as God's food (cf. Rom. 12:11; 2 Tim. 1:6). The morning signifies a new start for the burning. (Lev. 6:12, footnote 1)

The burning of the burnt offering laid a foundation for the sweetness of the peace offering. This indicates that our offering ourselves to God as a continual burnt offering (cf. Rom. 12:1) should be laid as a foundation for our sweet fellowship with God, signified by the burning of the fat of the peace offering. The burning of both the burnt offering and the peace offering signifies that both our absoluteness for God and our enjoyment of the Triune God should be a matter of burning. (Lev. 6:12, footnote 2)

I would like to say a word to the young people who have the heart to serve the Lord full time. I must tell you that hardships await you and that there is no future for you on earth. You will have nothing earthly on which to rely for your security and for your human living. You may feel that you will be very useful to God, but in the end you will be ashes. Everyone wants to be somebody, but if you would serve the Lord Jesus full time, you must prepare yourself to be nobody, even to be ashes.

The result of our being a burnt offering will be something that carries out God's New Testament economy....What we do must result in the building up of the Body of Christ, which is a miniature of the coming New Jerusalem.

What we are doing is actually extraordinary, but to the worldly people it is nothing. To them what we are doing is ashes. However, God has a high regard for these ashes. Eventually these ashes will become the New Jerusalem. (*Life-study of Leviticus,* pp. 208, 211)

Further Reading: Life-study of Leviticus, msgs. 9-10, 23

Enlightenment and inspiration: _____

_____

_____

Hymns, #1251

1   To Jerusalem we've come,
    We are through with Babylon,
    We have gathered to be one,
      Oh, glory be to God!
    Of the teachings we're bereft,
    All opinions we have left,
    Spirit from the soul is cleft,
      In the local churches now.

      Hallelujah! Hallelujah!
      We are all in one accord
      For the building of the Lord.
      Hallelujah! Hallelujah!
      We are living in the local
        churches now!

2   That recovery may proceed
    Real priests are what we need—
    Those who live in Christ indeed,
      Oh, glory be to God!
    Saturated with the Lord,
    They have Christ as their reward.
    These the building work afford
      In the local churches now.

3   And the kingship we must see
    With divine authority—
    To this rule we'll all agree,
      Oh, glory be to God!
    To the Spirit we'll submit
    For the church's benefit—
    This is His prerequisite
      In the local churches now.

4   We the altar must obtain,
    Have our all upon it lain.
    The burnt off'ring must be slain,
      Oh, glory be to God!
    This we never should dispute,
    For the church be absolute,
    All that's otherwise uproot
      In the local churches now.

5   The foundation now is laid—
     Oh, what glory doth pervade!
     We are all with joy arrayed,
        Oh, glory be to God!
     Let us raise a mighty shout—
     They will hear us far without,
     And the enemy we'll rout
        In the local churches now.

Composition for prophecy with main point and sub-points: _____

_____

_____

_____

_____

_____

_____

_____

_____

_____

_____

_____

_____

_____

_____

_____

_____

_____

_____

_____

_____

_____

_____

_____

The Recovery of the Church
as God's House and God's City
as Portrayed in Ezra and Nehemiah

Scripture Reading: Ezra 7:6-10, 21, 27-28; 8:21-23; 10:1;
Neh. 1:1-11; 2:4, 10, 17-20; 3:1-6; 4:4-5, 9; 5:10, 14-19;
8:1-4, 8-9, 14

Day 1 I. The recovery of a remnant of the children of
Israel from Babylon to Jerusalem for the rebuilding of the temple and the city signifies
the Lord's recovery of a remnant of the church
out of today's division and confusion back to
the original ground of oneness for the building up of the church as the house of God and
the kingdom of God (Rev. 17:1-6; 18:2, 4a):

A. God's people need to be recovered out of Babylon
back to the unique ground of oneness (Deut. 12:5,
11-14; Psa. 133; Rev. 1:11).

B. God's people need to be recovered back to the
enjoyment of the unsearchably rich Christ as the
all-inclusive Spirit, typified by the good land
(Eph. 3:8; Gal. 3:14; Deut. 8:7-10; Col. 1:12; 2:6-7).

Day 2 C. In the recovery of the church we are building up
the Body of Christ, the temple of God, the house
of God (Eph. 4:11-16; 1 Cor. 3:9-17).

D. In the recovery of the church we are living the
kingdom life to reign in life in the reality of
God's kingdom (Rom. 14:17; 5:17; cf. Matt. 5:3, 8;
6:6, 14-15, 20-21; 7:13-14).

E. This fulfills God's original intention to have a
corporate man to express Him in His image and
to represent Him with His dominion (Gen. 1:26).

Day 3 II. The Lord raised up Ezra to strengthen and
enrich His recovery (Ezra 7:6-10):

A. Ezra was a priest and also a scribe, one who was
skilled in the law of God; as such a person, Ezra
had the capacity to meet the need (v. 21):

       1. A priest is one who is mingled with the Lord and saturated with the Lord; Ezra was this kind of person (8:21-23).

       2. Ezra was a man who trusted in God, who was one with God, who was skilled in the Word of God, and who knew God's heart, God's desire, and God's economy (7:27-28; 10:1).

       3. Ezra was one with the Lord by contacting Him continually; thus, he was not a letter-scribe but a priestly scribe (Neh. 8:1-2, 8-9).

       4. Ezra spoke nothing new; what he spoke had been spoken already by Moses (Ezra 7:6; Neh. 8:14).

B. In the Lord's recovery we need Ezras, priestly teachers who contact God, who are saturated with God, who are one with God and filled with God, and who are skillful in the Word of God; this is the kind of person who is qualified to be a teacher in the Lord's recovery (Matt. 13:52; 2 Cor. 3:5-6; 1 Tim. 2:7).

Day 4   C. Ezra reconstituted the people of Israel by educating them with the heavenly truths so that Israel could become God's testimony (Neh. 8:1-4, 8):

       1. God's intention with Israel was to have on earth a divinely constituted people to be His testimony; in order for God's people to be His testimony, they had to be reconstituted with the word of God (Isa. 49:6; 60:1-3).

       2. After the return from captivity, the people were still unruly, for they had been born and raised in Babylon and had become Babylonian in their constitution:

         a. The Babylonian element had been wrought into them and constituted into their being (Zech. 3:3-5).

         b. After they returned to the land of their fathers to be citizens of the nation of Israel, they needed a reconstitution.

       3. There was the need of teaching and recon-

stitution to bring the people of God into a
culture that was according to God, a culture
that expressed God; this kind of culture requires a great deal of education (Neh. 8:8):

   a. Ezra was very useful at this point, for he
bore the totality of the heavenly and divine constitution and culture, and he
was one through whom the people could
be reconstituted with the word of God
(vv. 1-2).

   b. Ezra could help the people to know God
not merely in a general way but according to what God had spoken (v. 8).

4. In order to reconstitute the people of God,
there was the need to educate them with
the word that comes out of the mouth of God
and that expresses God (Psa. 119:2, 9, 105,
130, 140):

   a. To reconstitute the people of God is to
educate them by putting them into the
word of God so that they may be saturated with the word (Col. 3:16).

   b. When the word of God works within us,
the Spirit of God, who is God Himself,
through the word spontaneously dispenses
God's nature with God's element into our
being; in this way we are reconstituted
(2 Tim. 3:16-17).

Day 5

5. As a result of being reconstituted through
the ministry of Ezra, Israel (in type) became
a particular nation, a nation sanctified and
separated unto God, expressing God (Isa.
49:6; 60:1-3; Zech. 4:2):

   a. They were transfused with the thought
of God, with the considerations of God,
and with all that God is; this made them
God's reproduction.

   b. By this kind of divine constitution, everyone became God in life and in nature; as a

result, they became a divine nation expressing the divine character (1 Pet. 2:9).

   c. The returned captives were reconstituted personally and corporately to become God's testimony.

  D. In the Lord's recovery today, we need Ezras to do a purifying work and to constitute God's people by educating them with the divine truths so that they may be God's testimony, His corporate expression, on earth (2 Tim. 2:2, 15; 1 Tim. 3:15).

III. **The crucial point in the book of Nehemiah is that the city of Jerusalem with its wall was a safeguard and protection for the house of God within the city:**

  A. The rebuilding of the house of God typifies God's recovery of the degraded church, and the rebuilding of the wall of the city of Jerusalem typifies God's recovery of His kingdom; God's building of His house and of His kingdom go together (Matt. 16:18-19).

  B. The city of God is the enlarged, strengthened, and built-up church as the ruling center for God's reign in His kingdom; eventually, in God's economy the house of God becomes the holy city, the New Jerusalem, as God's eternal habitation and the ruling center of His eternal kingdom (Rev. 21:2-3, 22; 22:3).

  C. When we realize and enjoy Christ as our life, we have the church as the house of God; if we go further and realize His headship, the house will be enlarged to be the city, the kingdom of God (Eph. 1:22-23; 4:15; Rev. 22:1).

Day 6 D. Nehemiah's aggressiveness shows us the need for the proper aggressiveness in the Lord's recovery today:

    1. The leaders of the Moabites and Ammonites were greatly displeased about Nehemiah's seeking the good of the children of Israel; these descendants of the impure increase of

Lot hated and despised the children of Israel
(Neh. 2:10, 19; cf. Ezek. 25:3, 8).

2. In relation to the mocking, despising, and reproach of these opposers, Nehemiah was very
   pure and aggressive, not cowardly (Neh. 2:17-20;
   3:1-6; cf. Acts 4:29-31; 1 Thes. 2:2; 2 Tim. 1:7-8).

3. It is the aggressive ones who receive help
   from God; like Nehemiah, the apostle Paul
   was allied with God and realized God's as-
   sistance in this alliance (Acts 26:21-22).

4. Nehemiah's aggressiveness, as a virtue in his
   human conduct, shows that our natural capacity, ability, and virtues must pass through
   the cross of Christ and be brought into resurrection, into the Spirit as the consummation of the Triune God, to be useful to God in
   the accomplishing of His economy.

5. Nehemiah did not live in his natural man but
   in resurrection; he was a pattern of what a
   leader among God's people should be; he was
   aggressive (cf. Neh. 2:1-8), but his aggressiveness was accompanied by other characteristics:

   a. In his relationship with God he was one
      who loved God and also loved God's in-
      terests on the earth, including the Holy
      Land (signifying Christ), the holy tem-
      ple (signifying the church), and the holy
      city (signifying the kingdom of God) (cf.
      2 Tim. 3:1-5).

   b. As a person who loved God, Nehemiah
      prayed to God to contact Him in fellow-
      ship; for the rebuilding of the wall, Nehe-
      miah stood on God's word and prayed
      according to it (Neh. 1:1-11; 2:4; 4:4-5, 9).

   c. Nehemiah trusted in God and even be-
      came one with God; as a result, he became
      the representative of God (5:19; cf. 2 Cor.
      5:20).

  d. In his relationship with the people, Ne-
     hemiah was altogether unselfish, with-
     out any self-seeking or self-interest; he
     was always willing to sacrifice what he
     had for the people and for the nation
     (Neh. 4:18; 5:10, 14-19; 13:27-30).
E. The great and high wall of the holy city is for our
   separation unto God, the protection of God's
   interests, and the expression of God:
   1. The function of the wall of the city is to sep-
      arate, to sanctify, the city unto God from all
      things other than God, thus making the city
      the holy city (Rev. 21:2a, 10b; 1 Pet. 1:15-16;
      2 Cor. 6:14—7:1):
      a. The wall of the holy city, the New Jerusa-
         lem, is built with jasper, and the founda-
         tions of the wall of the city are adorned
         with every precious stone (Rev. 21:18-20):
         (1) By our growth in the divine life in
             Christ as the precious stone (1 Pet.
             2:4), we are transformed into pre-
             cious stones (1 Cor. 3:12a).
         (2) Precious stones indicate transforma-
             tion; the more we are transformed, the
             more we are separated (Rom. 12:2).
      b. While the transformation work of the
         Spirit is going on in the divine life, we,
         the transformed precious stones, are being
         built up together to be one complete wall
         with its foundations (1 Cor. 3:6-12a).
   2. The function of the wall of the city is to pro-
      tect the interests of the riches of God's di-
      vinity on the earth and the attainments of
      Christ's consummation; we must put out the
      pure truth from the Word for this protec-
      tion (cf. John 17:17).
   3. The function of the wall of the city is to
      express God; God's appearance is like jas-
      per, and the jasper wall signifies that the

whole city, as the corporate expression of God in eternity, bears the appearance of God (Rev. 4:3; 21:18).

Morning Nourishment

Deut.   ...To the place which Jehovah your God will choose,...
12:5   to His habitation,...there shall you go.
11-12   Then to the place where Jehovah your God will
        choose to cause His name to dwell, there you shall
        bring...your burnt offerings and your sacrifices,
        your tithes and the heave offering of your hand and
        all your choice vows which you vow to Jehovah.
        And you shall rejoice before Jehovah your God...

Recovery means the restoration or return to a normal condition after a damage or a loss has been incurred. When we speak of the recovery of the church, we mean that something was there originally, that it became lost or damaged, and that now there is the need to bring that thing back to its original state. Because the church has become degraded through the many centuries of its history, it needs to be restored according to God's original intention. Concerning the church, our vision should be governed not by the present situation nor by traditional practice but by God's original intention and standard as revealed in the Scriptures.

The recovery of the church is typified by the return of the children of Israel from their captivity (Ezra 1:3-11)....The entire history of the nation of Israel is a full type, an all-inclusive type, of the church. The nation of Israel began with the exodus.... Eventually, the people of Israel crossed the Jordan and entered into Canaan, the good land. After conquering the people and gaining the land, they built the temple....However,...mainly due to the failure of Solomon, the temple was destroyed, and the children of Israel were taken to Babylon as captives. (*The Conclusion of the New Testament*, pp. 2447-2449)

Today's Reading

Spiritually speaking, the church, due to its degradation, has been in captivity. God's people have been divided, scattered, and carried away from the proper ground of unity to a wrong ground. In the Old Testament type, the children of Israel were centered around Jerusalem, but later they were scattered and carried away to many places, in particular, to Babylon. This portrays the situation among many of today's Christians. In a very real sense, the believers today are more scattered than the children of Israel were. Therefore, we need to be recovered. We need not only revival but also recovery.

The recovery of the children of Israel was not only from Babylon but back to Jerusalem, the God-ordained unique ground. Jerusalem was the place the Lord had chosen (Deut. 12:5). Jerusalem, therefore, was the center for God's people to worship Him, and this unique center preserved the unity of the people of God. Without such a center, after the children of Israel had entered the good land, they would have been divided. Foreseeing this problem, God repeated the commandment again and again concerning the place of His choosing (Deut. 12:5, 11, 13-14). The people of Israel had no right to choose their own place to worship....God's choice became the center of the gathering of His people, and this is the unique ground of unity. For this reason, it was necessary for God's people in the Old Testament to be brought back to Jerusalem, the unique ground ordained by God.

Today's Babylon has not only captured God's people but also robbed all the riches from God's temple. The vessels, signifying the riches of Christ, have been carried away. This is the reason that in Roman Catholicism and in the Protestant denominations very little is said, if anything, concerning the unsearchable riches of Christ (Eph. 3:8). The believers are not encouraged to eat Christ, to drink Christ, to feast with Christ, to enjoy Christ in full. The reason there is little or no enjoyment of the riches of Christ is that all the vessels in the temple have been carried away by Babylon the Great. Now the Lord wants to recover the experience of the riches of Christ. He wants not only to call His faithful people out of Babylon and back to the proper church life but also to recover and bring back all the different aspects of Christ which have been lost. (*The Conclusion of the New Testament,* pp. 2449, 2451-2453)

Further Reading: The Conclusion of the New Testament, msg. 230

Enlightenment and inspiration: _____

_____

_____

_____

Morning Nourishment

Ezra   Thus says Cyrus the king of Persia, All the king-
1:2-3 doms of the earth has Jehovah the God of heaven
       given to me; and He has charged me to build Him a
       house in Jerusalem, which is in Judah. Whoever
       there is among you of all His people, may his God
       be with him; and let him go up to Jerusalem, which
       is in Judah, and let him build the house of Jehovah
       the God of Israel—He is God—who is in Jerusalem.

The recovery of the church is also typified by the rebuilding of
the temple of God, the house of God, in Jerusalem after the return
of God's people from Babylon. Ezra 1:3 says, "Whoever there is
among you of all His people, may his God be with him; and let him
go up to Jerusalem,…and let him build the house of Jehovah
the God of Israel…." Verse 5 goes on to say, "Then the heads of the
fathers' houses of Judah and Benjamin and the priests and the
Levites rose up, even everyone whose spirit God had stirred up to
go up to build the house of Jehovah, which is in Jerusalem." These
verses indicate that the recovery is not only a matter of going back
to Jerusalem with the vessels of the temple of God but also of
rebuilding the temple of God, which had been destroyed. (*The
Conclusion of the New Testament*, p. 2453)

Today's Reading

The recovery of the church is typified in the Old Testament
by the rebuilding of the city of Jerusalem (Neh. 2:11, 17). After
the recovery of the building of the temple, there was still the
need to build up the city. Without the city, there would have been
no protection for the temple. The temple, the place of the Lord's
presence, needed protection. The wall of the city was the defense
to the temple.

This also is an aspect of the type that we must apply in the
New Testament. Ephesians 2:19 and 1 Timothy 3:15 speak of the
church as the house of God. But in the last two chapters of Revelation, there is a city, and in this city there is no temple (Rev. 21:22),
because the city has become the enlargement of the temple.

Eventually, the whole church becomes the city. Because the temple has become the city, Revelation 21:22 tells us that there is no temple in the city of New Jerusalem. The city is the tabernacle, the dwelling place (Rev. 21:2-3). Hence, the city is the enlargement of the temple, the development of the house, to the uttermost.

The building of the house and the city is the center of God's eternal purpose. This building is actually the mingling of God with man. The church, therefore, is the mingling of divinity with humanity. When this mingling is enlarged and consummated to the fullest extent, that is the city. The city, then, eventually becomes the mutual building, the mutual habitation, of God and man, for God dwells in us and we dwell in God. This is the universal, eternal mingling of God with man. On a small scale, this is the house, and on a large scale, it is the city.

Finally, the recovery of the church involves the establishing of the kingdom life. This is indicated by Paul's word in Romans 14:17. "The kingdom of God is not eating and drinking, but righteousness and peace and joy in the Holy Spirit." This verse reveals that the kingdom of God is the living of the church. According to the context of Romans 14, the kingdom is today's church life. The reality of the church life is the kingdom. Romans 12 speaks of the Body life and Romans 14 of the kingdom life. This indicates that, according to Romans, the kingdom life is the reality of the Body life.

The kingdom of God as the living of the church is righteousness, peace, and joy in the Holy Spirit. When the authority of God's kingdom operates in us, righteousness, peace, and joy will characterize our daily life. To have such a living is to establish the kingdom life as typified in the book of Nehemiah by the rebuilding of the city of Jerusalem. Therefore, in the recovery of the church, we are building up the church as God's house and city. (*The Conclusion of the New Testament*, pp. 2453-2454, 2496)

Further Reading: The Conclusion of the New Testament, msg. 234

Enlightenment and inspiration: _____

_____

_____

_____

Morning Nourishment

Ezra   **This Ezra went up from Babylon, and he was a**
7:6-7   **scribe skilled in the law of Moses, which Jehovah**
       the God of Israel had given; and the king granted
       him all his request according to the hand of Jeho-
       vah his God upon him. Some of the children of
       Israel and some of the priests, and the Levites and
       the singers and the gatekeepers and the temple
       servants also went up to Jerusalem...

By the time Ezra returned, everything was recovered, but there was the need of strengthening and enrichment. The remnant of the people who returned was still small; the number needed to be increased, so Ezra brought back a good number. Today we really need more Ezras. The number we have today in the Lord's recovery is still too small; we need some Ezras to come back from Babylon to strengthen the recovery in number. So many priests, leaders, Levites, singers, and gatekeepers are still there in Babylon. They must be for the Lord's recovery. They may have been born in Babylon, but they were not born for Babylon. They were saved in the denominations, but they were not saved for the denominations; they were saved for the Lord and His recovery. (*CWWL, 1969,* vol. 2, "The Recovery of God's House and God's City," p. 372)

Today's Reading

The first return from Babylon to Jerusalem was initiated by God (Ezra 1:1, 5). The second return was initiated by Ezra, who went to the king and appealed to him to grant his request. Ezra realized that the first return was not perfect, not complete. He realized that there was the need for someone who was skilled in the law of God and who knew God's heart, God's desire, and God's economy, to help the people to know God not merely in a general way but according to what God had spoken. Ezra had such a capacity, so he volunteered to go to the king and to request a decree from the king permitting the Jews to return to the land of their fathers. (Ezra 7:6, footnote 1)

Ezra was a priest, a descendant of Aaron, and he was also a

scribe. The scribe in the Old Testament equals the teacher in the New Testament....The prophet is one who speaks directly from God, and the teacher is one who teaches the things spoken by the prophet....Haggai and Zechariah were prophets because they spoke directly from God. What was spoken by Haggai was new; it was never revealed to anyone else. Zechariah's message is even more marvelous. He said that Christ is the shoot, the foundation stone with seven eyes, and the topstone....Zechariah was not a teacher but a prophet, speaking from God's instant, present, up-to-date inspiration. Ezra spoke nothing new. What he spoke had been already spoken by Moses. He was a scribe and a teacher. But according to the principle in God's recovery, we do not need an old teacher, but a priestly teacher. Ezra was also a priest.

A priest is one who is mingled with the Lord, saturated with the Lord, feeding upon the Lord, and breathing Him in all day long. Whatever he speaks is just the Lord Himself. This is exactly what the teachers in the Lord's recovery must be. Ezra was this kind of person. He proclaimed a fast, and he fasted; he was simply one with the Lord by contacting the Lord continually. He was not a letter-scribe, but a priestly scribe.

He put his trust in the Lord. This is the kind of person who is qualified to be a teacher in the Lord's recovery....Mere knowledge does not build; it kills. It is the priestly teacher who builds. This is the kind of person who can strengthen the recovery with an increase of numbers and enrich it with the rich experiences of Christ. Praise the Lord there are such Ezras, and I have full assurance that the Lord is going to bring in more and more Ezras—those who are one with God, saturated with God, filled with God, and skillful in the work of God. These persons are the right ones to bring in a good number of returned captives and to bring more riches of Christ into the recovery of the Lord. (*CWWL, 1969,* vol. 2, "The Recovery of God's House and God's City," pp. 374-375)

Further Reading: CWWL, 1969, vol. 2, "The Recovery of God's House and God's City," chs. 1-3, 5-8

Enlightenment and inspiration: _____

_____

_____

Morning Nourishment

Neh.   And all the people gathered as one man....And Ezra
8:1-3 the priest brought the law before the assembly....
       And he read in it....And the ears of all the people
       were *attentive* to the book of the law.
7-8   ...And the Levites helped the people understand
       the law;...and they read in the book, in the law of
       God, interpreting and giving the sense, so that
       they understood the reading.

In order to be reconstituted, we need to come back to God by
coming back to His law, that is, His word (Neh. 8). Suppose a
fallen person wants to come back to God. If he would come
back to God, he must come back to God's word. No one can
come back to God without coming back to His word.

God's word reconstitutes us. We all have our own kind of disposition and habitual behavior, but God is able to reconstitute
us through His word. This is why we need to read the Bible.
God's word gradually changes our mind and our way of think-
ing. The word of God is one with the Spirit (Eph. 6:17). When
the word of God works within us, the Spirit, through the word,
spontaneously dispenses God's nature with God's element into
our being. We may not even be aware that such a dispensing is
taking place within us. By this way we are reconstituted. (*Life-
study of Nehemiah*, p. 17)

Today's Reading

The constitution of a person provides the foundation for the
constitution of a nation. A proper nation is not merely an organization but also a constitution.

Most of those who had returned to Jerusalem from the captivity in Babylon had been born not in Israel but in Babylon,
and they were raised in Babylon. The Babylonian element had
been wrought into them and constituted into their being.
Therefore, after they returned to the land of their fathers to be
citizens of the nation of Israel, they needed a reconstitution.
Ezra was very useful at this point, for he was one through

whom the people could be reconstituted with the word of God.

God's intention with Israel was to have on earth a divinely constituted people to be His testimony....Under Ezra and Nehemiah the returned people of Israel were collectively constituted by and with God through His word to be a nation as God's testimony. (*Life-study of Nehemiah*, pp. 18, 17-18)

[After the return from captivity], the people were still unruly for they had become Babylonian in their constitution. Therefore, there was the need for an Ezra, a priest who served God, and also a scribe, a scholar, who was skilled in the Word of God, skilled in the law of Moses (Ezra 7:6, 11). He bore the totality of the heavenly and divine constitution and culture. Ezra called the people together and confessed not only his own sin but also the sin of Israel, to bring them back to the Word of God. (*Life-study of Ezra*, p. 33)

In order for God to have a house and a kingdom on the earth, three sections of work were needed. First, there was a need for some of the captivity to come back from Babylon to Jerusalem to lay a foundation for the formation of a nation. This required a strong government, a strong administration. Second, there was the need of teaching and education to bring the people of God into a culture that was according to God. Such a culture was not an Egyptian kind nor a Canaanite kind nor a Babylonian kind but was God's kind, a culture that expressed God. This kind of culture required a great deal of education. Third, there was the need to constitute the nation organically. This section of the work was concerned with the constitution of God's people.

In our usage, the word constitution refers to something organic which has a number of elements. If the government of a country is constituted not only organizationally but also organically, that government will not be lifeless. On the contrary, such a government will be something that is living and organic. (*Life-study of Nehemiah*, pp. 9-10)

Further Reading: Life-study of Ezra, msgs. 1, 4-5; *Life-study of Nehemiah*, msgs. 2-4

Enlightenment and inspiration: _____

_____

_____

_____

Morning Nourishment

Neh. Thus I cleansed them from everything foreign. And
13:30 I appointed duties for the priests and the Levites,
      each in his work.
Psa. There is a river whose streams gladden the city of God,
46:4-5 the holy place of the tabernacles of the Most High.
      God is in the midst of her; she will not be moved...
Rev. And have made them a kingdom and priests to our
5:10 God; and they will reign on the earth.

In order to reconstitute the people of God, there is the need
to educate them with the word that comes out of the mouth of
God, which expresses God. This means that to reconstitute the
people of God is to educate them by putting them into the Word
of God that they may be saturated with the Word.

The Israelites had been in Egypt for at least four hundred
years. During those years they must have been constituted with
Egyptian learning. Then they were brought to Babylon for sev-
enty years. Zerubbabel, Ezra, and Nehemiah were all born and
raised among the Babylonians. After the people of Israel returned from Babylon, they mixed themselves with the Canaan-
ites. Thus, the Israelites were constituted with the Egyptian,
Babylonian, and Canaanite culture. Nevertheless, they returned
to be the testimony of God. But how could a people with a constitution of Egyptian, Babylonian, and Canaanite culture be God's
testimony, the expression of the God-man? Such a people were
not the God-men. How could they express God? In order to be the
testimony of God, His expression, they needed to be re-educated
in the Word of God. (*Life-study of Nehemiah,* p. 32)

Today's Reading

Before Nehemiah came back, the nation of Israel was a mess.
The duties of the priests were not certain, and no one was taking
care of the Levites and the serving ones. The singers were there,
but no one had opened the way for them to sing and to be formed
into companies. Nehemiah, with the help of Ezra, totally reconstituted the nation. Then Israel became a particular nation, a nation

sanctified and separated unto God, expressing God. They were transfused with the thought of God, with the considerations of God, and with all that God is, making them God's reproduction. Everyone became God in life and in nature by this kind of divine constitution. As a result, they became a divine nation on earth expressing the divine character. They were reconstituted personally and corporately to be God's testimony. The returned captives became God's testimony through the reconstitution which took place under the leadership of Nehemiah.

The crucial point of the book of Nehemiah is that the city of Jerusalem was a safeguard and protection for the house of God, which was in the city. This signifies that the house of God as His dwelling and home on the earth needs His kingdom to be established as a realm to safeguard His interest on the earth for His administration, to carry out His economy. The rebuilding of the house of God typifies God's recovery of the degraded church, and the rebuilding of the wall of the city of Jerusalem typifies God's recovery of His kingdom. God's building of His house and His building of His kingdom go together (Matt. 16:18-19). The house of God on the earth needs His kingdom to safeguard the house and to carry out His eternal economy. (*Life-study of Nehemiah,* pp. 33, 2)

The king in Psalm 45 typifies Christ as the King; the city in this psalm, and often in the Bible as a whole, signifies a kingdom. As the King, Christ needs a city in which to rule and reign. The city of God is the enlarged, strengthened, and built-up church as the ruling center for God's reign in His kingdom. The church as the house of God (23:6; 26:8; 27:4; 36:8; 1 Tim. 3:15) must be enlarged to become the church as the city, the kingdom, of God (Rev. 5:9-10). Eventually, in God's economy the house of God becomes the holy city, New Jerusalem, as God's eternal habitation and the ruling center of His eternal kingdom (Rev. 21:2-3, 22; 22:3). (Psa. 46:4, footnote 2)

Further Reading: Life-study of Nehemiah, msgs. 1, 5

Enlightenment and inspiration: _____

_____

_____

_____

Morning Nourishment

Neh.   ...The God of heaven Himself will make us prosper;
2:20   therefore we His servants will rise up and build...
Acts   Having therefore obtained the help which is from
26:22   God, I have stood unto this day, testifying both to
        small and great, saying nothing apart from the
        things which both the prophets and Moses have
        said would take place.

The leaders of the Moabites and Ammonites were greatly displeased about Nehemiah's seeking the good of the children of Israel (Neh. 2:10). The Moabites and the Ammonites, descendants of sons born of Lot, hated and despised the children of Israel.

[Nehemiah's] answer [v. 20] indicates that Nehemiah was very aggressive. He surely was not cowardly. Anyone who is cowardly cannot be a servant of God....Nehemiah trusted in God by praying that God would return their reproach to themselves. Thus the Jews built the wall, and all the wall was joined together to half its height, for they had a heart to work (4:4-6). Today, no matter how much we may be mocked and despised, we should have a heart to build and should be aggressive....In a very real sense, God will help those who help themselves. If you do not help yourself, God will not help you. According to history, God does not help the cowardly. It is the aggressive ones who have received help from God. (*Life-study of Nehemiah*, pp. 3-5)

Today's Reading

Nehemiah's aggressiveness, as a virtue in his human conduct, shows that our natural capacity, natural ability, and natural virtues must pass through the cross of Christ and be brought into resurrection, that is, into the Spirit as the consummated Triune God (John 11:25; 1 Cor. 15:45), to be useful to God in the accomplishing of His economy.

Nehemiah was one who lived not in his natural man but in resurrection. He was aggressive, but his aggressiveness was accompanied by other characteristics. In his relationship with God, he was one who loved God and also loved God's interests on the earth, including the Holy Land (signifying Christ), the holy temple (signifying the church), and the holy city (signifying the kingdom of God). As a person who loved God, Nehemiah prayed to God to contact Him in fellowship (Neh. 1:4; 2:4b; 4:4-5, 9). Furthermore, Nehemiah trusted in God and even became one with God. As a result, he became the representative of God. In his relationship with the people, Nehemiah was altogether unselfish; with him, there was no self-seeking or self-interest. He was always willing to sacrifice what he had for the people and for the nation (5:10, 14-19). (Neh. 2:3, footnote 1)

The first function [of the holy city's wall and its foundations (Rev. 21:12a, 14)] is to separate, to sanctify, the city unto God from all things other than God, thus making the city the holy city (21:2a, 10b).

The second function of the wall of the holy city with its foundations is to protect the interest of the riches of God's divinity on the earth and the attainments of His consummation. What are the riches of God's divinity, which need to be protected? Today God's divinity has been mocked. Some say that it is a heresy to believe that we are born of God to be His children and that we are God's family and have become God in life and in nature but not in the Godhead. To oppose this great truth is to mock the interest of the riches of God's divinity on the earth....We must put out the pure truth from the Word to protect the interest of the riches of God's divinity.

The third function of the wall is to express God. God's appearance is like jasper and the light of the New Jerusalem is like jasper, so the whole city will express God [Rev. 21:11]....Today, the function of the Body of Christ which consummates in the New Jerusalem is to express Christ. (*The Application of the Interpretation of the New Jerusalem to the Seeking Believers*, pp. 32-33, 35)

Further Reading: The Application of the Interpretation of the New Jerusalem to the Seeking Believers, msg. 3; CWWL, 1984, vol. 3, "God's New Testament Economy," ch. 36

Enlightenment and inspiration: _____

_____

_____

_____

Hymns, #1248

1 Recall how David swore,
"I'll not come into my house,
Nor go up to my bed,
Give slumber to mine eyelids,
Until I find a place for Thee,
A place, O Lord, for Thee."
Our mighty God desires a home
Where all His own may come.

2 How blinded we have been,
Shut in with what concerns us;
While God's house lieth waste—
Lord, break through, overturn us;
We'll go up to the mountain,
Bring wood and build the house;
We'll never say, "Another day!"
It's time! We'll come and build!

3 O Lord, against these days,
Inspire some for Your building,
Just as in David's day—
A remnant who are willing
To come and work in Your house,
Oh, what a blessed charge!
Your heart's desire is our desire—
We come, O Lord, to build.

4 Within those whom You'd call
Put such a restless caring
For building to give all—
These times are for preparing;
The gates of hell cannot prevail
Against the builded church!
The hours are few, the builders too—
Lord, build, oh, build in us!

(Repeat the last four lines)

Composition for prophecy with main point and sub-points: _____

_____

_____

_____

_____

_____

_____

_____

_____

_____

_____

_____

_____

_____

_____

_____

_____

_____

_____

_____

_____

_____

_____

_____

_____

_____

_____

_____

_____

_____

_____

_____

_____

_____

The Recovery of the Church Life

Scripture Reading: Matt. 16:18; 18:17; Rev. 22:16; Eph.
2:21-22; 3:16-21; 1 Cor. 1:9

Day 1   I. **Before the Lord Jesus comes back, He will
fully recover the proper church life (Matt.
16:18; 18:17; Rev. 1:11; 22:16, 20):**
   A. Nothing touches the Lord's heart as much as the
   recovery of the church life.
   B. In this present age, before His coming back, the
   Lord must have the church life to shame His enemy.
   C. No matter what Satan does to damage the church,
   the Lord Jesus will return, and His church will
   be waiting for Him.

Day 2   II. **The church life is Christ lived out through us in
a corporate way (Gal. 2:20; Phil. 1:21a; 3:9-10):**
   A. The church life is a life in which we take Christ
   as our life and our person (Col. 3:4; 1 John 5:11-12;
   Gal. 2:20; Eph. 3:16-17).
   B. The Christian life is not a religious life; it is a life
   that is Christ Himself lived out through us (Gal.
   2:20; Phil. 1:21a).
   C. When we live Christ, He joins us together in oneness, and Christ will be lived out through us in a
   corporate way (Rom. 12:4-5).
   D. Christ Himself is our life, and He is the Spirit
   within us; the church life is Christ Himself realized as life and as the life-giving Spirit dwelling
   in us (Col. 3:4; 1 John 5:11-12; 1 Cor. 15:45b; 2 Cor.
   3:17).
   E. The way to practice the church life is to put ourselves and everything on the cross and take
   Christ as life; then we will be permeated and
   saturated by Christ and with Christ (Rom. 6:6;
   Gal. 2:20; Col. 3:4).

Day 3   F. We need to learn to be inward Christians who
   are being transformed for the practice of the

church life (2 Cor. 3:18; Rom. 12:2-21):

1. The church life is Christ Himself as the Spirit permeating, saturating, and transforming us (1 Cor. 15:45b; Eph. 3:16-17).

2. The church life is a transformed life, not a natural life; it is Christ Himself as the subjective Spirit living within us (Rom. 12:2).

3. The more we are transformed and filled with Christ, the more we will be living, real, and practical members of Christ and realize the genuine church life (Eph. 3:17; 2 Cor. 3:18).

4. If we are transformed, it will be easy for us to be joined, knit, and built up together with others; this is to be built up in the church life (Eph. 2:21-22).

III. **The genuine experience of Christ always issues in and requires the church life (1 Cor. 1:2, 9, 30; 2:2, 10; 5:7-8; 10:3-4; 12:12-13, 27):**

A. The more we experience Christ, the more something within requires that we live in the proper church life.

B. When we experience Christ in a genuine and living way, He will require us to get into the church life because the dispensing of Christ into us is for the producing of the church (Rom. 8:11; 12:2-21).

C. God dispenses Himself into us as everything for the purpose of gaining His corporate expression, which is the church (Eph. 3:16-21).

D. When we take Christ as our life, our person, and our everything, this Christ within us will require the proper church life; in fact, the Christ in us will become the church life.

IV. **The church life is a life of being headed up under the unique headship of Christ (1:10, 22-23; 4:15-16):**

Day 4   A. God is heading up His chosen ones to be the Body of Christ, with Christ as the Head (1:4, 22-23):

  1. The first step in the heading up of all things in Christ is for God to place His sons under the unique headship of Christ (vv. 5, 10).

  2. When the church takes the lead to be headed up under the headship of Christ, God has a way to head up all other things (vv. 22-23, 10).

 B. In the proper church life we are being headed up in Christ (1 Cor. 11:3):

  1. If we do not know what it is to be headed up in Christ, we cannot know the church (Eph. 1:10, 22-23).

  2. In the church life we are taking the lead to be headed up in Christ; for this we need to grow up into the Head, Christ, in all things (4:15-16).

V. Fellowship is the reality of the church life (1 Cor. 1:9; 10:16-17; Acts 2:42; 1 John 1:3, 7):

 A. This fellowship involves not only the oneness between us and the Triune God but also the oneness among all the believers (John 17:21-23; Eph. 4:3).

Day 5 B. The church is the fellowship, the communion, the co-participation, the mutual enjoyment of Christ (1 Cor. 1:9).

 C. Fellowship also implies a mutual flowing among the believers (1 John 1:3, 7):

  1. In the New Testament, fellowship describes the flowing both between us and the Lord and between us and one another (Phil. 2:1).

  2. The flow, the current, that we have in our spiritual fellowship involves both oneness and life; our fellowship is a flow of oneness.

  3. This fellowship, this mutual flowing, is the reality of the church life (1 Cor. 1:9, 2).

VI. The church life is the continuation of the divine glorification—the continuation of Christ being glorified by the Father with the divine glory (John 12:23-24; 13:31-32; 17:1, 5, 22; Acts 3:13):

A. Glory is the expression of the divine life and the divine nature (7:2; Eph. 1:17):
   1. If we live by the divine life and nature, we will express the divine glory (4:18; 2 Pet. 1:4).
   2. The more we live by the divine life and the divine nature, the more divine glory there will be in the church (Eph. 3:21).
   3. The expression of this glory is the glorification of the Lord Jesus.

Day 6   B. The divine glorification began with the resurrection of the Lord Jesus, and it is continuing today (Luke 24:26; Rom. 6:4; 2 Cor. 3:18; Eph. 3:21).

C. The church has been produced in this glorification, and it continues to grow in the divine glorification (John 14:2; 15:1, 4-5; 16:21).

D. Whatever the church does in the matter of fruit-bearing is a continuation of the divine glorification (15:8).

VII. **The church life is the corporate expression of Christ (Eph. 3:16-21; 4:16; 5:27):**
   A. The key to the church life as the expression of Christ is the spirit of the mind (4:23):
      1. If we live according to the spirit of the mind, there will be in the church life an expression of the divine character (v. 24; Col. 3:10).
      2. We will be a corporate people with the flavor of Christ and the expression of God.
   B. In our virtues of lowliness, meekness, long-suffering, and love, there should be the expression of Christ as the embodiment of the Triune God (Eph. 4:2-6).
   C. The church life must be filled with the aroma and flavor of Christ and with the character of God; such a living is the living of the Triune God through our humanity (Phil. 1:20-21a).
   D. For centuries the Lord has been longing for such a church life (Eph. 1:5, 9):
      1. We pray that before long this kind of church life will be fully practiced among us in the

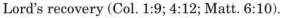

Lord's recovery (Col. 1:9; 4:12; Matt. 6:10).

2. May the Lord be satisfied by seeing such an expression of Himself through the recovery of the genuine church life throughout the earth.

Morning Nourishment

Matt. **And I also say to you that you are Peter, and upon**
16:18 **this rock I will build My church, and the gates of**
        Hades shall not prevail against it.
Rev. **Saying, What you see write in a scroll and send** *it* **to**
1:11 **the seven churches: to Ephesus and to Smyrna and**
        to Pergamos and to Thyatira and to Sardis and to
        Philadelphia and to Laodicea.

I have the assurance that before the Lord comes back, He will fully recover the proper church life. Many Christian teachers, however, do not believe that this is possible. According to them, we cannot have the church life in this age; they say the church life is possible only in the age to come. Those who hold this view say that we should not talk about the church, but simply love the Lord, preach the gospel, and help the believers to be spiritual. Many of those who take such a position are opposed to the Lord's present recovery. But in spite of all opposition, we have the assurance that the church life will be recovered in full in this age, not in the age to come. (*Life-study of Ephesians,* pp. 663-664)

Today's Reading

Nothing touches the Lord's heart as much as the recovery of the church life. This is His recovery today. The Lord desires to recover the church life so that He may have a people who have come out of every division, so that He may have a place for His name and for His habitation, and so that He may have the Holy of Holies in which and from which to speak to His people today. (*CWWL, 1977,* vol. 1, "The Kernel of the Bible," p. 229)

It is contrary to the Scriptures to say that the church life will be in the coming age. The next age will not be the age of the church; it will be the age of the kingdom. In this present age, before His coming back, the Lord must have the church life to shame the enemy. I believe that for centuries Satan, the enemy of God, has been challenging Christ concerning the church. Perhaps Satan has said to Him, "Where is Your church? Show me the church You have promised to build. Some of Your servants even teach that it is not possible to have the church life in this age." Perhaps Christ is saying to Satan, "Satan, look at the local churches on earth today. Consider how many of My people are testifying that it is possible to have the church life in this age. They are not only for the church life but are in the church life in a practical way."

I believe that in the coming years the Lord will spread the church life to England, Germany, France, and Italy. Furthermore, I believe that one day there will be a church in Rome and even in Jerusalem, where the church life began more than nineteen centuries ago. Acts 1:9-12 tells us that Christ ascended from the Mount of Olives, and Zechariah 14:4 reveals that Christ will return also to the Mount of Olives. In the same principle, the Lord began His church in Jerusalem and, I believe, will send the recovery of His church back to Jerusalem.

Concerning the recovery of the church life, the Lord Jesus cannot be defeated....No matter what Satan does to damage the church, the Lord Jesus will return, and His church will be waiting for Him. There may be a church in the city of Jerusalem. Perhaps the meeting hall will not be far from the Mount of Olives, the place from which He ascended and to which He will descend in His coming back. It would be a shame to the Lord Jesus to come back without having a church in Jerusalem ready for Him. The Lord will not suffer such a shame. For this reason, He is waiting for His recovery to spread to Europe and, ultimately, to Jerusalem.

We all need to enjoy Christ and to experience Him as the church-loving Christ. Because we also love the church, we are one with Him for the spread of His recovery throughout the world and back to Jerusalem. Oh, how Christ loves the church! He is in us as the church-loving Christ. His love for the church makes us willing to give our all for the recovery of the church life. (*Life-study of Ephesians,* pp. 664-666)

Further Reading: Life-study of Ephesians, msgs. 79-80

Enlightenment and inspiration: _____

_____

_____

_____

Morning Nourishment

Gal. I am crucified with Christ; and *it is* no longer I *who*
2:20 live, but *it is* Christ *who* lives in me; and the *life* which I
now live in the flesh I live in faith, the *faith* of the Son
of God, who loved me and gave Himself up for me.

Col. When Christ our life is manifested, then you also
3:4 will be manifested with Him in glory.

In the church life we do not need outward correction.
Instead, the church life is a life in which we all take Christ as
our life and person. The elders and the elderly sisters need to
help the saints to realize that their need is to take the Lord
Jesus as their person. The more all the saints do this, the more
they will experience the speaking of Christ as the life-giving
Spirit. This speaking will be to them the cleansing, purifying
water. This water will spread the element of Christ throughout
their being, and it will discharge all oldness. Eventually,...
[they] will no longer be bothered by problems with each other
but will grow together and be built up together. This is the
proper church life. (*Life-study of Ephesians,* pp. 467-468)

Today's Reading

What is the Christian life? What is the church life? The
Christian life is not a religious life; it is a life that is Christ Himself lived out through us. We must take Christ as life and live by
Him day by day. We need to love Him and be willing to be regulated, governed, and ruled by Him. Then we will be walking in
this living One, and we will be in the reality of the Christian
life. The church life is not something organized or something
regulated by teaching. The church life is Christ lived out
through us in a corporate way. You live Christ and I live Christ,
and this very Christ unites us together in oneness. Then together we have the corporate life of Christ expressed.

What is the life for us to practice the church, and what is the
proper way for us to practice the church life?...The burden today
is to meet the urgent need by helping us to see the life and the
way for the church practice. No doubt, we all would say that the

life for us to practice the church is Christ Himself. Many of us have the realization that we need Christ as our life, but very few realize that Christ as our life is for us to practice the church life.

There have been many teachings about life—the victorious life, the sanctified life, the exchanged life, the crucified life, the spiritual life, the divine life, the eternal life, and the life of Christ, the life of God. But it is hard to find a book telling us that this overcoming life, this spiritual life, the life of Christ, is for the church. This life is not just for victory or for sanctification. This life is not just for being spiritual, divine, and holy. This life is for a definite purpose, that is, for the building up of the church as the Body of Christ. Simply speaking, this life is for the church.

You have Christ as the Spirit in you. He is moving, acting, living, working, shining, regulating, and anointing within you. You need to follow this wonderful Spirit and cooperate with Him, go along with Him, and take Him as everything for yourself. Moreover, you need to learn the lesson of renouncing yourself. You can never practice the church life by the human life. If you do not learn the lesson of remaining on the cross all the time, there will be much trouble in your practice of the church life.... All of us have to go to the cross. If there are "you and I," there is no Body, no church. This is why Paul said, "I am crucified with Christ; and it is no longer I...but...Christ" (Gal. 2:20a).

We all have to see that the practice of the church life is not by bringing everyone into agreement with one another through discussions, talks, and negotiations with certain terms or conditions. Rather, the way to practice the church life is to put everyone and everything on the cross and to have everyone take Christ as life. Then we will be permeated and saturated by Christ and with Christ. Then we will be wholly, thoroughly, and absolutely a member of Christ from within to without. (*The Life and Way for the Practice of the Church Life,* pp. 66, 13, 73)

Further Reading: Life-study of Ephesians, msg. 55; *The Life and Way for the Practice of the Church Life,* chs. 7-9*

Enlightenment and inspiration: _____

_____

_____

_____

Morning Nourishment

Rom. And do not be fashioned according to this age, but
12:2 be transformed by the renewing of the mind that
you may prove what the will of God is, that which
is good and well pleasing and perfect.
  11 Do not be slothful in zeal, *but* be burning in spirit,
serving the Lord.

The church life is Christ Himself as the Spirit permeating, saturating, and transforming us. When we are fully transformed and are full of Christ, we will become the living, real, practical members of Christ. Then it will be easy for us to be joined, knit, and built up together with others. This is to be built up, not with something natural as wood, grass, and stubble but with something transformed as gold, silver, and precious stones (1 Cor. 3:12)....The church is organic, something growing up in life. (*The Life and Way for the Practice of the Church Life*, pp. 80-81)

Today's Reading

In order to have the church life, we need to go to the cross and take care of Christ, who is the wonderful Spirit within us. We need to take care of our inner feeling, inner guidance, inner shining, and inner registration. If we would go to the cross and realize Christ within us, we will be clear. All problems are solved by the cross. This is why in 1 Corinthians 2:2 the apostle Paul told the believers that he did not determine to know anything among them except Jesus Christ and this One crucified. The church life is a transformed life, not a natural life. It is Christ Himself, not as an objective doctrine but as the subjective Spirit living within us.

Do not try to change yourself outwardly. That is false. You have to be transformed from within to become a living member of the Body; then you will realize the genuine church life. This is what we need today. (*The Life and Way for the Practice of the Church Life*, p. 81)

The genuine experience of Christ always issues in and demands the church life. The more you experience Christ, the more something within requires that you live in the proper church life. Satan is subtle. Throughout the centuries he has concealed the real experience of Christ, making Christ altogether objective, an object of human belief and worship. But once we experience Christ in a genuine and living way, He will require us to get into the church life because the dispensation of Christ into us is for the producing of the church. God dispenses Himself into us as everything for the purpose of gaining His corporate expression, which is the church.

When we take Christ as our life, as our person, and as our everything, this Christ within us will require the proper church life. In fact, the Christ in us will become the church life. Christ both requires and becomes the church life. (*CWWL, 1975-1976,* vol. 3, "Young People's Training," pp. 326-327)

By the angelic rebellion and the human rebellion, the universe collapsed into a heap. This is the reason that today's human society and creation itself are such a mess. Everywhere there is nothing but rebellion....Nevertheless, God has purposed to bring in His administration to head up all things in Christ.

Does the body support the head or does the head uphold the body? The answer is that the head upholds the body. This is proved by the fact that if a person's head is cut off, the body falls to the ground....In like manner, the church life is a life of being headed up. If we truly want to have a glorious church, we must be willing to be headed up. All around us, at school, at work, and in the government, we see nothing but a state of collapse; nothing is headed up. But in the proper church life we are being headed up. This heading up in the church life is the beginning of God's heading up of all things. Under Christ and through the church, God will head up all things in the universe. This is the mystery of God's will. Ultimately, the mystery of God's will in the universe is to head up all things in Christ. (*Life-study of Ephesians,* p. 70)

Further Reading: CWWL, 1984, vol. 4, "Vital Factors for the Recovery of the Church Life," chs. 4-6; *Basic Principles for the Practice of the Church Life,* ch. 3

Enlightenment and inspiration: _____

_____

_____

_____

Morning Nourishment

Eph. Unto the economy of the fullness of the times, to
1:10 head up all things in Christ, the things in the heavens and the things on the earth, in Him.
4:15 But holding to truth in love, we may grow up into
Him in all things, who is the Head, Christ.

The first step is for God to bring His chosen ones, His sons, out
of the collapse and to place them under the headship of Christ.
Here, under the headship of Christ, we are outside of the heap
of the universal collapse, and we are over all things. Thus, the
church life must be a life of being headed up. In the church life it is
God's chosen ones, not the world leaders, the unbelievers, or the
animals, that are being headed up. God is heading up all His chosen ones to be the Body of Christ with Christ as the Head. Eventually, this Body with Christ as the Head will be the universal
Head over all things. (*Life-study of Ephesians*, pp. 76-77)

Today's Reading

Today we in the church are taking the lead to be headed up in
Christ. If we are not willing to be headed up in the church life, we
shall delay the heading up of all things. In fact, God will not have a
way to accomplish the heading up of all things in Christ if we, the
chosen ones, are not willing to be headed up. But if we are willing
for this, God will say with joy, "These are the pioneers who are taking the lead to be headed up. They are pioneering the way for Me to
head up all things in Christ." When the church takes the lead to be
headed up in Christ, God has a way to head up all other things.

Many Christians are talking about the church, but in their talk
the word *church* has become meaningless. In the book of Ephesians, however, the church means a great deal. But if you do not
know what it is to be headed up in Christ, you cannot know what
the church is. The church is not a heap of fallen people who are still
in the collapse. The church is the heading up of God's chosen ones
under the headship of Christ. In contrast to the genuine church, today's Christianity is a heap. Wherever you go in Christianity, you
see one heap after another. The reason there are so many heaps in

the denominations or in the independent Christian groups is that, just as in human society, there is no heading up. But in the proper church life we are being headed up in Christ.

Today we in the church life are taking the lead to be headed up in Christ. For this we need to grow in life and have the light of life. (*Life-study of Ephesians,* pp. 77-80)

I would encourage you all to seek the experience and the enjoyment of the fellowship of God's Son. The more we enjoy the co-participation in this fellowship, the better the church life will be. We need to enjoy this fellowship both at home and in the meetings. Then we shall not be troubled by opinions, gossip, or different teachings, for we shall not care for anything other than the practical co-enjoyment of the all-inclusive Christ who is to us the Spirit, the resurrection, and the Triune God. This fellowship is the reality of the church. Thus, we must seek to experience this fellowship all the time. Then we shall enjoy Christ in the church.

It is not easy to give an adequate definition of the fellowship of the Son of God. This matter is altogether wonderful. This fellowship involves not only the oneness between us and the Triune God, but also the oneness among all the believers. Furthermore, it implies enjoyment—our enjoyment of the Triune God, the Triune God's enjoyment of us, and also the enjoyment which the believers have with one another. In this fellowship we enjoy the Triune God, and the Triune God enjoys us. Moreover, we enjoy all the believers, and all the believers enjoy us. What a wonderful, universal, mutual enjoyment! We have been called into something which is termed the fellowship of God's Son. This fellowship is universal and mutual. The mutuality of this fellowship is not only between the believers and the Triune God but also among the believers themselves. (*Life-study of 1 Corinthians,* pp. 103-104, 30-31)

Further Reading: CWWL, 1978, vol. 3, "Crucial Principles for the Proper Church Life," ch. 3; *CWWL, 1978,* vol. 2, "Crucial Principles for the Christian Life and the Church Life," ch. 6; *Life-study of Ephesians,* msgs. 8-10

Enlightenment and inspiration: _____

_____

_____
_____

Morning Nourishment

1 Cor. God is faithful, through whom you were called into
1:9 the fellowship of His Son, Jesus Christ our Lord.
Eph. To Him be the glory in the church and in Christ
3:21 Jesus unto all the generations forever and ever.
Amen.

The church is the fellowship, the communion, the co-participation, the mutual enjoyment, of Christ. This Christ is now the resurrection and the Spirit. If you have seen that the church life consists in this fellowship,...you will not be distracted from Christ by doctrines or practices. (*Life-study of 1 Corinthians*, p. 103)

Today's Reading

The word *fellowship* is used for the first time in Acts 2:42, where we are told that those who were saved and added to the church on the day of Pentecost continued steadfastly in the teaching and the fellowship of the apostles. The apostles had preached the gospel to them, and this gospel preaching brought them into something which the Bible calls fellowship.

I doubt that there is in any language an equivalent of the Greek word for fellowship, *koinonia*. This word implies oneness and also a mutual flowing among the believers. When we enjoy fellowship with one another, there is a flow among us....The flow, the current, we have in our spiritual fellowship involves both oneness and life. Our fellowship is a flow in oneness; it is an inter-communication among us as believers in Christ.

In the New Testament, fellowship describes both the flowing between us and the Lord and between us and one another. First John 1:3 says, "That which we have seen and heard we report also to you that you also may have fellowship with us, and indeed our fellowship is with the Father and with His Son Jesus Christ."...There is a flow, a current, vertically between us and the Father and the Son and horizontally between us and other believers. Praise the Lord that on earth today there is something called fellowship, a fellowship among the children of God and a fellowship of the children of God with the Triune God!

Since the day of Pentecost a current has been flowing horizontally among the believers. This flow crosses space and time. As far as time is concerned, this fellowship has been flowing from generation to generation. As far as space is concerned, this fellowship is worldwide; it flows among believers throughout the globe. Because we are in this one flow, we cannot be separated by space. No matter where we may be, we are all in the flow; that is, we are all in the one fellowship.

According to Paul's word in 1 Corinthians 1:9, we all have been called by God into this fellowship. Perhaps the best illustration of fellowship is the circulation of blood in the human body....Life depends on this circulation. Just as there is the circulation of blood in the human body, so there is a spiritual circulation, called the fellowship, in the Body of Christ....It is crucial for us to realize that in the Lord's recovery we are being brought back into this flow, into this fellowship. (*Life-study of 1 Corinthians*, pp. 124-125)

The sign of the Lord's glorification signifies many things. It signifies that the old creation has been terminated and also that the new creation has been germinated. Adam has been terminated, and the new man has come into being. It was through this glorification that the old man was done away with and that the new man has been brought forth. Therefore, in resurrection the new man was born with glory. Even in the church life today there is at least some amount of glorification.

We all need to be clear that glory is the expression of the divine life and the divine nature. If we live by the divine life and nature, we will express the divine glory....The more the saints live by the divine life and the divine nature, the more glorious the church life is, the more divine glory there will be in the church. The expression of this glory is the glorification of the Lord Jesus. (*CWWL, 1982*, vol. 2, "The Fulfillment of the Tabernacle and the Offerings in the Writings of John," p. 466)

Further Reading: Life-study of 1 Corinthians, msg. 11; The Issue of Christ Being Glorified by the Father with the Divine Glory, chs. 2-5

Enlightenment and inspiration: _____

_____

_____

_____

Morning Nourishment

John In this is My Father glorified, that you bear much
15:8 fruit and *so* you will become My disciples.
Eph. And *that* you be renewed in the spirit of your
4:23 mind.

The divine glorification continues today. This glorification began with the Lord's resurrection, and it is still going on. According
to our viewpoint, we may say that the delivery that brought forth
the Firstborn and the many brothers covers a long span of time,
thus far, more than nineteen hundred years. In the sight of God,
this delivery, although lengthy in time, is a matter of resurrection.

I believe that what the Lord has shown us concerning the divine glorification will help us to know what the church life is. The
church life is actually the multiplication, the propagation, of Christ.
This kind of church life is the divine glorification. The church has
been produced in this glorification, and it continues to grow in the
divine glorification. Whatever the church does in the matter of
fruit-bearing is a continuation of the divine glorification. As the
church spreads, this spreading is the fruit-bearing. For example,
fifteen years ago there were only a small number of saints in the
Lord's recovery in Europe. But now this number has increased.
This increase is a matter of fruit-bearing, and fruit-bearing is the
divine glorification. (*CWWL, 1982*, vol. 2, "The Fulfillment of the
Tabernacle and the Offerings in the Writings of John," pp. 474-475)

Today's Reading

When we are filled in spirit unto all the fullness of God and
honor our parents out of such an infilling, there will be the
expression of God in our relationship to our parents. Our
behavior will not be a mere human virtue; it will be a virtue
with the divine character and with the flavor of Christ. As we
honor our parents, there should be the sweet savor of Christ.
This is the expression of God through human virtue. Suppose a
young man honors his parents from a spirit filled unto all the
fullness of God. In this virtue there will be the divine character.
This is the expression of God in humanity.

This expression of God is absolutely different from mere ethical behavior. Although the followers of Confucius may attain a high ethical standard, there is no flavor of Christ in their virtue. I repeat, in our virtue there needs to be the character of God and the flavor and taste of Christ. Such a divine expression through human virtue is conveyed by the Greek word for holiness in Ephesians 4:24. The church life must be filled with such an expression of divine character through human virtue.

In our honesty and generosity there needs to be the expression of the divine character. There are two kinds of honesty and two kinds of generosity: an honesty and a generosity that are mere human virtues, and an honesty and a generosity that express the character of God. In the church life our honesty and generosity must have the flavor of Christ. As others contact us, they should not only have the sense that we are virtuous; they should be able to sense in our virtue the flavor of Christ and see the expression of the divine character.

The key to the church life is the spirit of the mind. If we live according to the spirit of the mind, there will be in the church life the expression of the divine character. Then we shall be a corporate people with the flavor of Christ and the expression of God. If we simply give others the impression that we are good, righteous, and kind, our church life is a failure. There must be in our goodness, righteousness, and kindness the expression of the Triune God. The church life must be filled with the aroma and flavor of Christ and with the character of God. Such a living is the living of the Triune God through our humanity. For centuries, God has been longing for such a church life. We pray that before long this kind of church life will be fully practiced among us in the Lord's recovery. May the Lord be satisfied by seeing such an expression of Himself through the corporate new man on earth! (*Life-study of Ephesians,* pp. 791-793)

Further Reading: CWWL, 1982, vol. 2, "The Fulfillment of the Tabernacle and the Offerings in the Writings of John," chs. 38, 51

Enlightenment and inspiration: _____

_____

_____

_____

Hymns, #1220

1   Remove the veils, Lord, from my heart;
     True revelation grant to me;
     A vision clear, O Lord, impart
     Of Thy recovery.

2   By revelation I perceive
     The pow'r that raised Christ from
        the dead;
     When I by faith this pow'r receive,
     I to the church am led.

3   Thy mighty pow'r has set me free
     From all the world's distracting things;
     An entrance to the local church
     This mighty power brings.

4   Once in the local church, I need
     To take Thee as my person, Lord;
     My outward man each day recede,
     My heart is for the Lord.

5   I take Thee as my person, Lord;
     I have been crucified with Thee.
     My inner man has been restored;
     I'm now indwelt by Thee.

6   When all Thy members self forsake,
     Thy glorious Body, Lord, is known;
     When of Thy person we partake,
     The one new man is shown.

7   The church life is the one new man
     In every local church expressed;
     Thy Body is a corporate man,
     One person manifest.

(Repeat the last two lines of each stanza)

Composition for prophecy with main point and sub-points: _____

_____
_____
_____
_____
_____
_____
_____
_____
_____
_____
_____
_____
_____
_____
_____
_____
_____
_____
_____
_____
_____
_____
_____
_____
_____
_____
_____
_____
_____
_____
_____
_____
_____
_____
_____
_____
_____

Jehovah's Commanded Blessing of Life
on Brothers Who Dwell Together in Oneness

Scripture Reading: Psa. 133—134

Day 1   I. **The unique ground of Jerusalem, the place**
           where the temple as God's dwelling place
           was built on Mount Zion, typifies the unique
           ground of God's choice, the ground of one-
           ness (Deut. 12:5; 2 Chron. 6:5-6; Ezra 1:2-3):
           A. In the ancient time all the Israelites came to-
              gether three times a year at Jerusalem; it was
              by this unique place of worship to God, Jerusa-
              lem, that the oneness of His people was kept for
              generations (Deut. 12:5; 16:16).
           B. In the New Testament the proper ground of one-
              ness ordained by God is the unique ground of
              one church for one locality (Rev. 1:11):
              1. The church is constituted of the universal
                 God, but it exists on earth in many local-
                 ities; in nature the church is universal in
                 God, but in practice the church is local in a
                 definite place, such as "the church of God
                 which is in Corinth" (1 Cor. 1:2):
                 a. "The church of God" means that the church
                    is not only possessed by God but has God
                    as its nature and essence, which are di-
                    vine, general, universal, and eternal (v. 2a).
                 b. The church "which is in Corinth" refers
                    to a church in a city, remaining in a defi-
                    nite locality and taking it as its standing,
                    ground, and jurisdiction for its adminis-
                    tration in business affairs, which is phys-
                    ical, particular, local, and temporal in
                    time (v. 2b).
              2. Without the universal aspect, the church is
                 void of content; without the local aspect, it
                 is impossible for the church to have any
                 expression and practice; the record con-
                 cerning the establishment of the church in

its locality is consistent throughout the New
Testament (Acts 8:1; 13:1; 14:23; Rom. 16:1;
1 Cor. 1:2; 2 Cor. 8:1; Gal. 1:2; Rev. 1:4, 11).

Day 2 II. **Psalm 133 is the praise of a saint, in his going
up to Zion, concerning Jehovah's commanded
blessing of life on brothers who dwell together in oneness; the blessing that is commanded whenever brothers are united under
the anointing is a "life forever," a full, free,
unceasing stream of life:**

A. The brothers' dwelling together in oneness is
likened to the inestimable goodness of the precious ointment on the head of Aaron and to the
incalculable pleasantness of the dew of Hermon
on the mountains of Zion (vv. 1-3):

1. As a person typified by Aaron, the church
as the one new man includes the Head with
the Body as the corporate Christ, the corporate priesthood (Eph. 2:15; 1 Pet. 2:5).

2. As a place typified by Zion, the church is the
dwelling place of God (Deut. 12:5-7, 11, 14,
18, 21, 26; Eph. 2:21-22; Rev. 21:3, 22).

B. The genuine oneness is constituted of the spreading ointment and the descending dew for the
gradual building up of Christ's Body in the divine dispensing of the Divine Trinity:

Day 3 1. Psalm 133 is equivalent to Ephesians 4; when
we are in the Body and are diligent to keep
the oneness of the Spirit, we have the anointing of the Spirit (vv. 3-6); the anointing
oil as the compound ointment is a type of the
processed Triune God, the all-inclusive compound Spirit (Exo. 30:23-25):

a. The compound Spirit is the ultimate consummation of the processed Triune God
with the divine attributes, the human
virtues, Christ's death with its effectiveness, and Christ's resurrection with its
power (Phil. 1:19).

b. We are in the oneness that is the processed
Triune God anointed, or "painted," into our
being (2 Cor. 1:21-22; 1 John 2:20, 27).

c. Day by day in the church life, all the ingredients of the divine and mystical compound ointment are being wrought into
us; through the application of these ingredients to our inward being, we are spontaneously in the oneness (Eph. 4:3-4).

Day 4

d. The ground of oneness is simply the processed Triune God applied to our being; the
anointing of the compound, all-inclusive
life-giving Spirit is the element of our oneness (v. 4; cf. John 4:24):

(1) If we act apart from the Spirit, who
is in our spirit, we are divisive and
lose the oneness (Eph. 4:3; cf. 1 Cor.
1:10; 2:14-15; 3:1).

(2) If we stay in the life-giving Spirit,
we keep the oneness of the Spirit
(cf. John 4:24; 1 Cor. 6:17).

e. The compound Spirit is not for those who
are individualistic; He is in and for the
Body and for the priestly service that builds
up the Body (Psa. 133:2; Exo. 30:26-31;
Phil. 1:19; Rom. 15:16; 1 Pet. 2:5, 9).

f. We receive the supply of the Spirit, the
supply of the Body, by the intercession
and fellowship of the members:

(1) When we are dry and have no way
to go on, we need other brothers and
sisters to intercede for us before we
can get through (Phil. 1:19; 1 Thes.
5:25; Job 42:8-10).

(2) We cannot live without the supply
of the Body; therefore, we must constantly avail ourselves of the fellowship of the Body (1 Thes. 3:8; 1 Cor.
10:16b; 1 John 1:3).

(3) If a man wants to see light, he has to enter the church, the sanctuary (Psa. 73:16-17; Matt. 5:14; Rev. 1:20).

Day 5

2. The dew of Hermon descending on the mountains of Zion signifies the descending, refreshing, watering, and saturating grace of life (1 Pet. 3:7), the Triune God as our life supply for our enjoyment (2 Cor. 13:14):

a. In typology Hermon signifies the heavens, the highest place in the universe (cf. Eph. 1:3; Matt. 17:1-2).

b. The mountains of Zion typify the local churches; there is one Zion, one church as one Body, but many mountains, many local churches (Rev. 1:11-12).

c. Grace is God in Christ as the Spirit experienced, received, enjoyed, and gained by us (John 1:16-17; 1 Cor. 15:10; Gal. 2:20; Rom. 5:2, 17, 21).

d. By remaining in the church life, we are preserved in the Lord's grace (Acts 4:33; 11:23).

e. By the grace we receive on the mountains of Zion, we can live a life that is impossible for people in the world to live (20:32; 2 Cor. 12:7-9).

f. The Christian living must be the living of grace, the experience of grace (v. 9; 2 Tim. 4:22):

(1) We have faith and love through the Lord's superabounding grace (1 Tim. 1:14).

(2) By grace we receive the salvation in life through Christ's resurrection and ascension (Eph. 2:5-8).

(3) We have obtained access into and stand in God's abounding grace (Rom. 5:2).

(4) In this grace we can enjoy God's eternal comfort and good hope (2 Thes. 2:16).

(5) We can come forward with boldness to the throne of grace to find grace for timely help (Heb. 4:16).

(6) We can receive God's abounding supply of grace (2 Cor. 9:8).

(7) We can constantly enjoy God's multiplying grace (1 Pet. 1:2b; 2 Pet. 1:2; Rev. 22:21).

(8) We can enjoy God's greater grace through humility (James 4:6; 1 Pet. 5:5).

(9) In our experience of the grace in God's economy, we enjoy the Lord's presence in our spirit (2 Tim. 4:22; cf. Luke 1:28, 30).

(10) We need to live out Christ as God's righteousness by the grace of God (Gal. 2:20-21).

(11) We need to experience the perfecting of the Lord's sufficient grace, Christ's overshadowing power, in our weakness (2 Cor. 12:9).

(12) By grace we can overcome the usurpation of temporal and uncertain riches and become generous in ministering to the needy saints (8:1-2).

(13) The God of all grace perfects, establishes, strengthens, and grounds us through our sufferings (1 Pet. 5:10).

(14) We need to be good stewards of the varied grace of God (4:10; Eph. 3:2).

(15) Our word should convey Christ as grace to others (4:29-30).

(16) We need to experience Christ as grace to be a surpassing one and to

labor abundantly for the Lord (1 Cor. 15:10).

(17) We need to receive the abundance of grace and of the gift of righteousness to reign in life (Rom. 5:17, 21).

g. The grace given to the local churches in the dark age of the church's degradation is for the believers who seek to answer the Lord's calling to be His overcomers (Rev. 1:4).

h. The grace of the Lord Jesus Christ dispensed to His believers throughout the New Testament age consummates in the New Jerusalem as the consummation of God's good pleasure in joining and mingling Himself with man for His enlargement and eternal expression (22:21).

3. In the church life we are daily anointed and graced; the anointing of the Spirit and the supply of grace make it possible for us to live in oneness (Eph. 1:13, 6).

Day 6

4. The more we experience Christ as the life-giving Spirit, the more our natural constitution and disposition are reduced; as they are reduced through our experience of the Triune God with His divine attributes, we are perfected into one (John 17:23; Eph. 4:1-3).

III. **As the conclusion to Psalm 133 and as the last of the Songs of Ascents, Psalm 134 is the praise of a saint, in his going up to Zion, concerning the charge and the blessing of the children of Israel to the serving priests in the house of God:**

A. This psalm indicates that the highest people, those who are in Zion, can bless everyone and teach everyone (vv. 1-2; cf. Gen. 47:10; 48:20; 49:28).

B. The blessing comes from Zion, from the highest peak, from the ones who have attained to the top, to the position of the overcomers; in every age and century God's blessing has come to the church because of the overcomers (Psa. 134:3; cf. Rev. 2:7).

Morning Nourishment

Deut. But to the place which Jehovah your God will choose
12:5 out of all your tribes to put His name, to His habitation, shall you seek, and there shall you go.
1 Cor. To the church of God which is in Corinth, to those who
1:2 have been sanctified in Christ Jesus, the called saints,
with all those who call upon the name of our Lord
Jesus Christ in every place, *who is* theirs and ours.

The return of Israel to Jerusalem from their captivity was crucial in four points: (1) it recovered the purpose of God's calling Israel
to make them His testimony according to His law (see footnote 1 on
Exo. 20:1); (2) it recovered the oneness of Israel on the unique
ground of Jerusalem (Deut. 12:5, 11-14); (3) it recovered Israel's enjoyment of the good land promised by God; and (4) it allowed God to
fulfill His intention of having His house built and His kingdom
established on the Satan-usurped earth in order to carry out His
eternal economy through Israel's participation in and enjoyment of
the good land. All the foregoing crucial points typify today's recovery of the church life, which is a recovery of the church out of captivity in the great Babylon (Rev. 17:1-6) back to the unique ground of
God's choice, the ground of oneness. (Ezra 1:1, footnote 1)

Today's Reading

The church is constituted of the universal God, but it exists
on earth in many localities, one of which was Corinth. In nature
the church is universal in God, but in practice the church is
local in a definite place. Hence, the church has two aspects: the
universal and the local. Without the universal aspect, the church
is void of content; without the local aspect, it is impossible for
the church to have any expression and practice. Hence, the
New Testament stresses the local aspect of the church also
(Acts 8:1; 13:1; Rev. 1:11; etc.). (1 Cor. 1:2, footnote 2)

"The church...in Corinth" (1 Cor. 1:2b) was a church in a
city, remaining in a definite locality and taking it as its standing, ground, and jurisdiction for its administration in business
affairs. As such, it was physical, particular, local, and temporal

in time. The church of God to whom Paul wrote was not in the heavens but in Corinth. Corinth was a very sinful, modern Greek city, which was famous for its fornication. However, the church remained in that locality for a local testimony of Christ. A local testimony of Christ is a part of the universal testimony of Christ. The universal testimony is composed of and constituted with the local testimonies. (*A Genuine Church*, p. 8)

[The church in Jerusalem] was the first church established in a locality (see footnote 1 on Acts 5:11) within the jurisdiction of a city, the city of Jerusalem. It was a local church in its locality, as indicated by the Lord in Matthew 18:17. It was not the universal church, as revealed by the Lord in Matthew 16:18, but only a part of the universal church, which is the Body of Christ (Eph. 1:22-23). The record concerning this matter (the establishing of the church in its locality) is consistent throughout the New Testament (Acts 13:1; 14:23;...1 Cor. 1:2; 2 Cor. 8:1; ...Rev. 1:11). (Acts 8:1, footnote 1)

First Corinthians 1:2 contains five qualifications for a genuine church....The church which is genuine is the church of God, it is the church in a locality, it is sanctified in Christ, and it is composed of the called saints. Verse 2e continues with the fifth qualification: "With all those who call upon the name of our Lord Jesus Christ in every place." This long phrase indicates that the church which is genuine is related with all the saints who call upon the name of the Lord Jesus Christ in every place around the globe.

Being related with all the saints keeps us from being sectarian, isolated, or divided. Regardless of their particular practices, we are related by God in Christ to every kind of Christian, and no matter where we are, we cannot be separated from them. Without this relationship we would become isolated and divided. If we have nothing to do with other believers, we are not a local church. Rather, we are a local sect, a local division. (*A Genuine Church*, pp. 10-11)

Further Reading: The Ground of the Church

Enlightenment and inspiration: _____

_____

_____

_____

Morning Nourishment

Psa. For Jehovah has chosen Zion; He has de-
132:13-16 sired it for His habitation. This is My resting
place forever; here will I dwell....I will abundantly bless its provision....Its priests I will
clothe with salvation, and its faithful ones
will shout with a ringing shout.

133:1 Behold, how good and how pleasant it is for
brothers to dwell in unity!

Psalm 133 is the praise of a saint, in his going up to Zion, concerning Jehovah's commanded blessing on brothers who dwell in
oneness. When Zion is built up and when God is resting there and
dwelling in Jerusalem, as depicted in Psalm 132, we have a place
where we can gather and where we can dwell together in oneness.
How good and how pleasant this is! (Psa. 133:1, footnote 1)

In Psalm 133 the believers' dwelling together in oneness is
likened to the inestimable goodness of the precious ointment on
the head of Aaron and to the incalculable pleasantness of the
dew of Hermon on the mountains of Zion. (Psa. 133:1, footnote 2)

The unity spoken of here is a picture of the genuine oneness
in the New Testament. This oneness is the processed and consummated Triune God mingled with the believers in Christ
(John 17:21-23). Since the Body of Christ is such a mingling (Eph.
4:4-6), the Body itself is the oneness. According to the picture in
this psalm, the genuine oneness is constituted of the spreading
ointment and the descending dew for the gradual building up of
the Body of Christ in the divine dispensing of the Divine Trinity.
(Psa. 133:1, footnote 3)

Today's Reading

[In Psalm 133] dwelling together in oneness is likened to two
things: to the precious ointment on the head of Aaron and to the
dew of Hermon on the mountains of Zion. These two adjectives
point to two aspects of oneness. The oneness is good and pleasant:
good as the precious ointment and pleasant as the descending dew.
Of these aspects, the first—Aaron—is a person, and the second—

Zion—is a place....The church has these two aspects....As a person, the church includes the Head with the Body. As a place, the church is the dwelling place of God. Elsewhere in the Bible we see that the church is the bride, the new man, and the war-rior. These, however, are aspects of the church as a person. Actually, the church has just two main aspects: the aspect of a person and the aspect of a dwelling place. Related to these two aspects of the church are the ointment and the dew.

[Verse 2] refers to the anointing oil described in Exodus 30. That anointing oil was a compound ointment formed by blending four spices with olive oil. Aaron, his sons, the tabernacle, and every-thing related to the tabernacle were anointed with this ointment. According to Psalm 133, this ointment, this compound anointing oil, was upon a person, Aaron....By contrast, the refreshing, water-ing, and saturating dew was on a place, the mountains of Zion.

Neither the anointing oil nor the saturating dew moved quickly. The dew did not fall down like rain; it descended, came down, in a gradual way. In like manner, the ointment did not actu-ally run down upon Aaron's beard; it spread upon his beard and then ran down to the hem of his garments....Gently and slowly, the ointment spread. In the same principle the dew came down upon the mountains of Zion....The genuine oneness is constituted of the spreading ointment and the descending dew.

Aaron [is] a type of Christ in His priestly ministry. As the High Priest, Christ served God, accomplished God's purpose, and ful-filled the desire of God's heart. However, in Psalm 133 Aaron typi-fies not only Christ Himself but Christ with His Body. This means that here Aaron typifies the corporate Christ, the Head with the Body....The church is thus a universal, great person with a num-ber of aspects: the aspects of the Body, the bride, the new man, and the warrior. All these aspects of the church are related to the per-son. (*The Genuine Ground of Oneness*, pp. 295-296, 303)

Further Reading: CWWL, 1979, vol. 2, "The Genuine Ground of Oneness," ch. 6

Enlightenment and inspiration: _____

_____

_____

_____

Morning Nourishment

Eph. Being diligent to keep the oneness of the Spirit in the
4:3-6 uniting bond of peace: one Body and one Spirit, even
as also you were called in one hope of your calling;
one Lord, one faith, one baptism; one God and Father
of all, who is over all and through all and in all.

In Ephesians 4:4-6 Paul lists seven aspects of oneness: one
Body, one Spirit, one hope, one Lord, one faith, one baptism,
and one God and Father. These verses also show the mysterious mingling of the Triune God with the Body of Christ. This
mingling is the oneness of the believers. The Spirit in verse 4 is
no doubt the compound, all-inclusive Spirit who is within the
Body and gives life to the Body. (*CWWL, 1979,* vol. 2, "The Genuine Ground of Oneness," p. 301)

Today's Reading

Psalm 133 is the key passage in the Old Testament concerning the anointing....[In verse 1 the] dwelling in unity is corporate; there is no barrier or separation. They have cast aside their
disunity, jealousy, and hatred....In this condition, they receive
God's anointing [v. 2]. When the oil flows down, those who are
under the head will spontaneously receive the oil. Psalm 133 is
equivalent to Ephesians 4. When we are in the Body and are diligent to keep the oneness of the Spirit, we have the anointing of
the Spirit. We have to come under the Head, and we have to live
in the Body before we can receive the anointing....In order for us
to receive the anointing, we must submit to the Head and live in
the Body....The more we live in the fellowship of the Body, the
more we enjoy the anointing of the Spirit. (*CWWN,* vol. 44, "The
Mystery of Christ," pp. 819-820)

Real oneness is the mingling of the processed God with the
believers. Although this is revealed in the New Testament, we do
not see in the New Testament the way to practice this oneness.
The way to practice this mingling is in Psalm 133. The ointment
in verse 2 is a type of the processed Triune God who today is
the all-inclusive compound Spirit. According to Exodus 30, the

anointing oil is a compound formed by blending four spices with a hin of olive oil. This compound typifies the all-inclusive Spirit who is the processed God for our enjoyment. In this compound Spirit we have not only divinity but also Christ's humanity, the effectiveness of His death, and the power of His resurrection. In other words, the compound Spirit is the processed God with the divine attributes, the human virtues, the effectiveness of Christ's death, and the power of Christ's resurrection. In the church life this compound Spirit is continually anointing us.

The ointment can be compared to paint, and the anointing to the application of the paint....As all these ingredients of the ointment are applied to us, we are "painted" with the processed Triune God and with all the elements in the compound ointment. The proper church life is a life in the oneness that is the mingling of the processed Triune God with the believers....We are in the oneness that is the processed Triune God "painted" into our very being....Day by day in the church life, all the ingredients of the divine ointment are being wrought into us. Through the application of these ingredients to our inward being, we are spontaneously in the oneness. We find it exceedingly difficult to be divisive or even dissenting. How good, lovely, and enjoyable is the oneness in the church!...We are one spontaneously because we have been "painted" with all the elements of the heavenly "paint."

The ground of oneness is simply the processed Triune God applied to our being....We are not in a oneness produced by adding together those who believe in Christ. In that kind of oneness it is just as easy to have subtraction as it is to have addition. However, once we have been brought into the oneness produced by the application of the processed Triune God to our being, it is very difficult to have any subtraction....The oneness in the churches in the Lord's recovery involves the application of the Triune God to our inward being. (*The Genuine Ground of Oneness,* pp. 297-299)

Further Reading: CWWN, vol. 44, "The Mystery of Christ," chs. 7, 10; *CWWL, 1979,* vol. 2, "The Genuine Ground of Oneness," chs. 7, 9

Enlightenment and inspiration: _____

_____

_____

_____

Morning Nourishment

Psa. Behold, how good and how pleasant it is for broth-
133:1-2 ers to dwell in unity! It is like the fine oil upon the
head that ran down upon the beard, upon Aaron's
beard, that ran down upon the hem of his garments.
Phil. For I know that for me this will turn out to salva-
1:19 tion through your petition and *the* bountiful supply
of the Spirit of Jesus Christ.

The oneness of the Spirit is the Spirit Himself. To keep, [safe-guard, and preserve by guarding] the oneness of the Spirit is to keep the life-giving Spirit. If we act apart from the Spirit, we are divisive and lose the oneness. If we stay in the life-giving Spirit, we keep the oneness of the Spirit. (Eph. 4:3, footnote 1)

Today's Reading

The ointment is not for individuals; it is for the Body. It cannot be experienced by those who are separate and detached from the Body. According to the picture in Psalm 133, the ointment is upon the head. Then it spreads to the beard and goes down to the hem of the garment. This indicates that if we are individualistic, we cannot experience the ointment....If we are one with the church, then we can properly contact the Lord alone at home. But if we separate ourselves from the church, our contact with the Lord will be altogether different. The reason is that the anointing oil is not for individualistic members; it is for the Head and the Body, even for the Head with the Body. (*CWWL, 1979*, vol. 2, "The Genuine Ground of Oneness," p. 299)

[In Philippians 1:19] the phrase *your petition* indicates the supply of the Body. Apparently Paul was in prison; actually he was in the Body. Imprisonment did not isolate him from the Body or cut him off from the supply of the Body. Paul had the clear sense within that he was in the Body and that the members of the Body were supplying him, supporting him, and standing with him.

In 1:19 Paul speaks first of the saints' petition, then of the bountiful supply of the Spirit....The reason Paul speaks of the supply of the Body before the bountiful supply of the Spirit is that the Spirit is upon the Body. Psalm 133 illustrates this: the ointment poured upon Aaron's head flowed down to the body. This portrays the fact that the ointment, the bountiful supply of the compound Spirit, is upon the Body. Paul realized that he was not the whole Body but just a member of the Body. As a member, he needed the Body's supply. If the Body would be exercised to supply him, the bountiful supply of the Spirit would come to him through the Body.

We may often ask a brother to pray for us. But even if he prays for us and we pray for him, this prayer may have little effect. The reason for this lack of effectiveness is that in praying we may stand apart from the Body. Whenever we stand apart from the Body as we pray, even our prayer will be dry, and our intercession will be ineffective. The anointing is not upon us individually; it is upon the Body.

According to Exodus 30, the compound ointment was for the anointing of the tabernacle and the priests. It is very important to realize that the compound Spirit, the Spirit of Jesus Christ, is for the Body, God's tabernacle, and for God's service, the priesthood. Because so many Christians today are cut off from the Body and from the priestly service, it is extremely difficult for them to share the bountiful supply of the Spirit.

Paul lived in the Body. Although he was a wonderful apostle, he still needed the prayers and petitions of the saints. This is a clear indication that Paul had a right relationship with the Body. Furthermore, Paul also shared in the priesthood. Because he was in the Body, the tabernacle, and because he was part of the priesthood, God's service, he was in a proper position to receive the flow of the ointment which is upon the Body....If we are one with the church and stay in the priestly service, we enjoy the rich anointing of the all-inclusive Spirit. Even a little praying or calling on the name of the Lord, perhaps simply saying Amen, causes us to enjoy this anointing. (*Life-study of Philippians*, pp. 286-287, 291-292)

Further Reading: Life-study of Philippians, msg. 33

Enlightenment and inspiration: _____

_____

_____

_____

Morning Nourishment

Psa.   Like the dew of Hermon that came down upon the
133:3   mountains of Zion. For there Jehovah commanded
         the blessing: life forever.
1 Tim.   And the grace of our Lord superabounded with
1:14   faith and love in Christ Jesus.
Rom.   ...Those who receive the abundance of grace and
5:17   of the gift of righteousness will reign in life through
         the One, Jesus Christ.

[The dew in Psalm 133:3 typifies] the fresh and refreshing grace of God, which comes to us through God's fresh compassions (Lam. 3:22-23; cf. Prov. 19:12). This grace—the Triune God processed and consummated to be our life supply for our enjoyment (John 1:14, 16-17; 2 Cor. 13:14)—waters us. Hermon, a high mountain, signifies the heavens, the highest place, from which the dew descends. The anointing of the Spirit (Psa. 133:2) and the supply of grace make it possible for us to live in oneness. (Psa. 133:3, footnote 1)

The many mountains of the one Zion typify the many local churches as the components of the unique universal church. In the local churches we daily enjoy the Lord's grace as the descending dew. (Psa. 133:3, footnote 2)

Today's Reading

In typology Hermon signifies the heavens, the highest place in the universe, and the dew signifies the grace of life (1 Pet. 3:7). Without the New Testament, it would be difficult for us to realize that dew signifies grace. Every Epistle written by Paul opens with a word about grace and closes with some mention of grace.

Strictly speaking, *grace* is a New Testament term. When used in the Old Testament, it has the meaning of "favor." According to John 1:17, grace came through Jesus Christ. When the Word became flesh and tabernacled among us, grace came also. This means that grace came with the incarnated God. Before the incarnation of Christ, grace had not come.

The anointing oil and the watering dew are found in the church.

Here we experience the anointing, the "painting," of the processed Triune God. Simultaneously, we enjoy the processed God as grace, as the life supply for our enjoyment. By this grace we can live a life that is impossible for people in the world to live....Such a living is possible through the grace we receive on the mountains of Zion. (*The Genuine Ground of Oneness,* pp. 306-307, 310)

The Christian living must be the living of grace, the experience of grace....Grace is God's embodiment—Christ. Hence, the grace experienced by the believers is Christ, the embodiment of God.

Grace is Christ. All the spiritual experiences of a Christian should be experiences of Christ as grace. In our experience of the grace in God's economy, first, we have faith and love through the Lord's superabounding grace (1 Tim. 1:14)....Faith and love are products of the Lord's grace. Through faith we receive the Lord, and through love we enjoy the Lord whom we have received. We have neither faith nor love, but when we allow the Lord to come into us, both faith and love from the Lord as grace come into us.

In their experience of the grace in God's economy, the believers also receive the salvation in life in Christ's resurrection and ascension (Eph. 2:5-8). This salvation is a salvation in life....This salvation is the resurrected and ascended Christ becoming our grace.

The believers' experience of the grace in God's economy enables them to obtain access into and stand in God's grace (Rom. 5:2a). Today we are not under the law but under the grace in God's economy. This grace is God Himself.

We reign in life by receiving the abundance of grace and of the gift of righteousness. This is grace reigning in life unto eternal life (Rom. 5:17b, 21b)....We have received righteousness objectively, but we still need to continually receive the abundance of grace so that we can reign in life subjectively....This is to overcome. This is grace reigning unto eternal life. (*The Law and Grace of God in His Economy,* pp. 48, 35-37, 41)

Further Reading: The Law and Grace of God in His Economy, chs. 2-4

Enlightenment and inspiration: _____

_____

_____

_____

Morning Nourishment

John 17:23 I in them, and You in Me, that they may be perfected into one, that the world may know that You have sent Me and have loved them even as You have loved Me.

Psa. 134:1-3 Bless Jehovah now, all you servants of Jehovah who stand by night in the house of Jehovah. Lift up your hands in the sanctuary, and bless Jehovah. May Jehovah, who made heaven and earth, bless you from Zion.

[In John 17:23] the words *I, them,* and *You* refer respectively to Christ, the believers, and the Father. The Son is in the believers, and the Father is in the Son. This is the mingling of the [processed] Triune God with the believers. As a result of such a mingling, we may be perfected into one.

On the day we believed in Christ, we came into this oneness. However, we still have problems with our natural man, our natural constitution, and our natural disposition. But the more we experience Christ as the life-giving Spirit, the more all these natural elements are reduced. As they are reduced through our experience of the Triune God, we are perfected into one.

The oneness revealed in the Bible is not a matter of adding the believers together to form a harmonious unit. Such a concept of oneness is natural and superficial....Oneness is the mingling of the processed Triune God with the believers. Having seen this oneness as it is unfolded in John 17 and Ephesians 4, let us now consider [Psalm 134 as the conclusion of] Psalm 133. (*CWWL, 1979,* vol. 2, "The Genuine Ground of Oneness," p. 295)

Today's Reading

By the close of Psalm 132 God enters into His rest, and we obtain satisfaction in the habitation of God. Hence, following that, we have the church life in Psalm 133. Psalm 134 now is a conclusion to that wonderful church life presented in Psalm 133. (*CWWL, 1969,* vol. 3, "Christ and the Church Revealed and Typified in the Psalms," pp. 176-177)

As the last of the Songs of Ascents, Psalm 134 is the praise of the saint in His going up to Zion concerning the charge and the blessing of the children of Israel to the serving priests in the house of God. This psalm indicates that the highest people, those who are in Zion, can bless everyone and teach everyone.

"Bless Jehovah now, / All you servants of Jehovah / Who stand by night in the house of Jehovah. / Lift up your hands in the sanctuary, / And bless Jehovah" (vv. 1-2). This is the charge of the children of Israel to the serving priests. Although these priests are serving in the house of God, they are lower than the ones in Zion. Thus, those in Zion can give such a charge to these servants of Jehovah.

"May Jehovah, who made heaven and earth, / Bless you from Zion" (v. 3). Here we see that the blessing comes from Zion, that is, from the highest people. If you read the history of the church, you will see that in every age and century God's blessing has come to the church because of the overcomers. Whenever there are some overcomers, there will be God's blessing. God always blesses His people from Zion, from the highest peak, from the ones who have attained to the top, to the position of the overcomers. From this position God blesses all His people. (*Life-study of the Psalms*, pp. 485-486)

Then the last verse of Psalm 134 is the answer, the reply, of the priests to the people: "May Jehovah, who made heaven and earth, / Bless you from Zion." God's servants bless Him in His house, and God blesses His people from Zion. This little psalm means that we all must fellowship and communicate in this way. After a good meeting, after a rich enjoyment of Christ, some of us may say, "Bless the name of the Lord." Then others may answer, "The Lord bless you from Zion." How blessed! Let us try it. This is a good fellowship, a good communication, a good conclusion, to a meeting of the church. (*CWWL, 1969*, vol. 3, "Christ and the Church Revealed and Typified in the Psalms," p. 177)

Further Reading: Life-study of the Psalms, msg. 42; *CWWL, 1969,* vol. 3, "Christ and the Church Revealed and Typified in the Psalms," ch. 21

Enlightenment and inspiration: _____
_____
_____
_____

Hymns, #1339

1 Behold, how good and how pleasant it is
   For brethren to dwell together in unity!
   Behold, how good and how pleasant it is
   For brethren to dwell together in unity!

   It is like the precious ointment upon
      the head
   That ran down upon the beard,
   Even Aaron's beard,
   That went down to the skirts of his
      garments.

2 Behold, how good and how pleasant it is,
   For brethren to dwell together in unity!

   It is like the precious ointment upon
      the head
   That ran down upon the beard,
   Even Aaron's beard,
   That went down to the skirts of his
      garments.

3 As the dew of Hermon,
   And as the dew that descended
   Upon the mountains of Zion:
   For there the Lord commanded the blessing,
   Even life forevermore.

Composition for prophecy with main point and sub-points: _____

_____

_____

_____

_____

_____

_____

_____

_____

_____

_____

_____

_____

_____

_____

_____

_____

_____

_____

_____

_____

_____

_____

_____

_____

_____

_____

_____

_____

_____

_____

_____

_____

_____

_____

The Status of the Church— the Body of Christ

Scripture Reading: Eph. 1:22-23; 4:16; Rom. 12:4-5; 1 Cor. 12:12-13; 14:26

Day 1   I. **Ephesians 1:22 and 23 reveal that the church is the Body of Christ:**

A. The church is not an organization but an organic Body constituted of all the believers, who have been regenerated and have God's life, for the expression of the Head (John 3:3, 5-6, 15; 1:12-13; 1 John 5:11-12).

B. The Body is the fullness of the Head, and the fullness is the expression of the Head (Eph. 1:22-23).

C. Christ, as the One who fills all in all, needs the Body to be His fullness; this Body is the church to be His fullness (3:10; 1:22-23; 4:10).

D. The church is the Body of Christ, and Christ is the Head of the church (Col. 1:18; 2:19); hence, the church and Christ are one Body, the mysterious, universal great man (3:10-11; Eph. 2:15; 4:24), having the same life and nature:

1. Christ is the life and content of the Body, and the Body is the organism and expression of Christ (Col. 3:4; 1:18; 2:19; Rom. 12:4-5).

2. As the Body, the church receives everything from Christ; therefore, everything of Christ is expressed through the church (Eph. 1:22-23; 3:8, 10).

3. The two, Christ and the church as His Body, are mingled and joined as one, with Christ being the inward content and the church being the outward expression (vv. 16-21).

II. **We need to see clearly how the Body of Christ has been formed:**

A. In Christ's resurrection the processed and consummated Triune God has been wrought into His chosen people (John 20:22; 1 Cor. 15:45b; 6:17; 1 Pet. 1:3).

B. In Christ's ascension the all-inclusive, compound Spirit, as the consummation of the processed Triune God, descended upon His chosen people (Luke 24:49; Acts 1:8; 2:4, 32-33).

C. Within them God's chosen, redeemed, and regenerated people have Christ as the embodiment of the processed and consummated Triune God, and upon them they have the consummated Spirit (John 20:22; Luke 24:49).

D. In this way the believers in Christ become the Body of Christ, an organism produced through the mingling of the processed and consummated Triune God with the transformed tripartite man (1 Cor. 12:13, 27; Eph. 5:30).

Day 2 III. **The reality of the Body of Christ is the Spirit of the reality of the Triune God (4:4; John 14:17; 15:26; 16:13-14; 1 John 5:6):**

A. Reality refers to the real condition of persons and things.

B. The Body of Christ is the church, and all its reality is the Spirit of the reality of the consummated Triune God (Eph. 1:22-23; 4:16; John 16:13-14):

1. The reality of the processed Triune God is His consummated Spirit of reality (14:17; 15:26; 16:13; 1 John 5:6).

2. The reality of all that the Triune God is, has, and can do is this Spirit of reality (John 16:13-14).

3. The reality of the death and resurrection through which the Triune God has passed is also in the Spirit of reality (Eph. 2:5-6).

4. The Spirit of reality makes everything of the processed Triune God a reality in the Body of Christ (1 John 5:6; Eph. 4:4).

5. All that the Triune God is, including righteousness, holiness, life, light, power, grace,
and all the divine attributes, are realized
by the Spirit of reality to be the real attributes of the Body of Christ (Rom. 15:16b;
14:17; Eph. 3:16-17a).

6. These attributes have been realized in the
church by the Spirit in the Body of Christ;
the church therefore possesses the reality
of the divine attributes (4:24; Col. 3:12-15).

7. All that the Triune God in Christ experienced, including incarnation, crucifixion,
and resurrection, are likewise realized by
the Spirit of reality to be the real experiences of the Body of Christ (Rom. 6:3-6;
Phil. 3:10).

Day 3   IV. **The church as the Body of Christ is the corporate Christ (1 Cor. 12:12):**

A. In 1 Corinthians 12:12 *the Christ* is not the individual Christ but the corporate Christ, the Body-
Christ, composed of Christ Himself as the Head
and the church as His Body, with all the believers as its members:

1. The Bible considers Christ and the church
as one mysterious Christ; the two have been
joined together to become one mysterious
Christ, the Body-Christ (Eph. 5:32).

2. All the believers of Christ are organically
united with Him and constituted of His life
and element to become His Body, an organism, to express Him (Rom. 12:4-5; Col. 3:4,
15).

B. As a vine includes not only the stalk but also
the branches, so the corporate Christ, the Body-
Christ, includes not only Christ Himself but also
the members of Christ's Body, who are the members of Christ, parts of Christ (John 15:1, 4-5;
Eph. 5:30; 1 Cor. 12:27; Rom. 12:5):

1. Christ is the element, the factor, that makes us parts of Him (Col. 3:10-11).
2. In order to be parts of Christ, members of His Body, we must have Christ wrought into our being (Gal. 1:15-16; 2:20; 4:19; Eph. 3:16-17).
3. The church can be the Body of Christ, the corporate Christ, only as the members are constituted of Christ, possessing His life and nature (Col. 3:4, 10-11).

C. The baptism into the one Body has positioned us all to drink of the one Spirit, and by drinking of the Spirit, we are constituted to be the Body, the corporate Christ (1 Cor. 12:13):
1. By drinking the Spirit, we experience the dispensing of the Divine Trinity into our being and are constituted to be the Body.
2. The more we drink the one Spirit, the more the divine element becomes our constituent to make us the one Body, the Body-Christ (vv. 12-13).

Day 4 V. **For the building up of the Body of Christ, we need to practice the scriptural way to meet and to serve (14:26; Heb. 10:24-25):**
A. Without the biblical way for us to meet and to serve, the way that is shown in the New Testament, the Lord's words concerning the building up of the church cannot be fulfilled (Matt. 24:35; 16:18; Eph. 4:11-16).
B. If 1 Corinthians 14:26 and Hebrews 10:24-25 are not fulfilled, there is no way for the building up of the church as the Body of Christ.
C. The scriptural way to meet and to serve, with all the saints functioning as living members of the Body of Christ, is versus the traditional way, the natural way, to meet and to serve, which is in the principle of the clergy-laity system (Rev. 2:6, 15):
1. The traditional way fits man's natural and

fallen condition, is religious, and accommodates the dead man's taste (cf. Matt. 25:23-30).

Day 5   2. The traditional way binds and annuls the
organic function of the living members of
Christ and chokes and kills the members
of Christ (Rev. 2:6).

3. The scriptural way is spiritual, fits the taste
of the living and spiritual man, and requires us to be living and in the spirit (John
4:23-24; Acts 13:52; Gal. 5:16; Rom. 8:4;
2 Tim. 1:6-7).

Day 6   4. The scriptural way is able to develop the
organic ability and function of the members
of Christ and able to build up the Body of
Christ (Eph. 4:12-16).

D. The Lord desires to recover the organic building
up of the Body of Christ:

1. The organic building up of the Body of Christ
is the increase of the Triune God in the
believers for their growth in Christ (Col.
2:19; Eph. 4:15-16).

2. The Lord desires to recover the church meetings in mutuality with all prophesying (speaking for the Lord) for the building up of the
church; prophesying is the excelling way to
dispense the riches of Christ into God's people for the organic building up of the Body of
Christ (1 Cor. 14:4b, 12, 31; cf. Matt. 16:18).

Morning Nourishment

Eph. **And He subjected all things under His feet and**
1:22-23 **gave Him** *to be* **Head over all things to the church,**
which is His Body, the fullness of the One who fills
all in all.

Ephesians 1:22 and 23 reveal that the church is the Body of Christ....The church is not an organization but an organic Body constituted of all the believers, who have been regenerated and have God's life, for the expression of the Head. The Body is the fullness of the Head, and the fullness is the expression of the Head. Christ, as the One who fills all in all, needs the Body to be His fullness. This Body is His church to be His expression. (*The Conclusion of the New Testament,* p. 2245)

Today's Reading

The church is the Body of Christ, and Christ is the Head of the church (Col. 1:18). Hence, the church and Christ are one Body, the mysterious, universal great man, having the same life and nature. Christ is the life and content of the Body, and the Body is the organism and expression of Christ. As the Body, the church receives everything from Christ; everything of Christ, therefore, is expressed through the church. The two, Christ and the church, are mingled and joined as one, with Christ being the inward content and the church, the outward expression.

As the embodiment of the processed Triune God becoming the life-giving Spirit, the Lord breathed the Spirit into His disciples essentially. Then He ascended to the heavens and passed through a process involving the Father with the Spirit, a process that involved the mystery of the Triune God. Having received from the Father the promise of the Spirit, He poured out this Spirit upon His believers. Actually, what He poured out was Himself as the embodiment of the Triune God consummated into the all-inclusive compound Spirit as the totality of the processed Triune God. Now the embodiment of the processed Triune God becoming the life-giving Spirit is within the disciples, and the consummated, all-inclusive Spirit is upon them.

This is a mingling of the processed Triune God with His chosen, called, redeemed, regenerated, and transformed tripartite people to become one entity—the Body of Christ.

Now we can see clearly how the Body of Christ was formed. First, in resurrection the processed Triune God has been wrought into His chosen people. Then, in Christ's ascension, the all-inclusive, compound Spirit as the consummation of the processed Triune God descended upon His chosen people. As a result, within them they have the embodiment of the processed Triune God, and upon them they have the consummated Spirit. In this way they become the Body of Christ, an entity produced through the mingling of the processed Triune God with the transformed tripartite man. This is the church.

We all need to see that the Body of Christ is the totality of the processed Triune God mingled with transformed, tripartite man. This mingling, which will consummate in the New Jerusalem, is completed in three stages. The first stage extends from God's incarnation to Christ's breathing Himself in resurrection as the processed Triune God into God's chosen people to make them intrinsically the constituent for the formation of the Body. This was completed on the day of the Lord's resurrection. After this, the Lord ascended to the heavens. In the heavens there was a transaction between the Father and the Son concerning the Spirit. This is the reason we are told clearly that the ascended Christ received of the Father the promise of the Spirit. Hence, in ascension the Son received of the Father the promised Spirit. Then the Lord poured Himself out as the consummated, all-inclusive, compound Spirit upon the believers. This was the completion of the second stage. Now a third stage is needed for the increase of the Body unto all the fullness of God, unto the fullness of the One who fills all in all. (*The Conclusion of the New Testament,* pp. 2245-2246, 2251-2252)

Further Reading: The Conclusion of the New Testament, msgs. 210-211

Enlightenment and inspiration: _____

_____

_____

_____

Morning Nourishment

John   *Even* the Spirit of reality, whom the world cannot
14:17   receive, because it does not behold Him or know
        Him; *but* you know Him, because He abides with
        you and shall be in you.
Eph.   One Body and one Spirit, even as also you were
4:4   called in one hope of your calling.

The reality of the Body of Christ [is] the Spirit of the reality of
the Triune God....Reality refers to the real condition of persons
and things. The Body of Christ is the church today, and all of its
reality is the Spirit of the reality of the consummated Triune
God. The reality of the processed Triune God is His consummated Spirit of reality (John 14:17; 15:26; 16:13; 1 John 5:6). The
reality of all that the Triune God is, has, and can do is simply this
Spirit of reality. The reality of the death and resurrection which
the Triune God passed through is also this Spirit of reality. (*A
Thorough View of the Body of Christ,* p. 31)

Today's Reading

Furthermore, this Spirit of reality makes everything of the processed Triune God a reality in the Body of Christ (John 16:13-15). It is
this same Spirit of reality who makes all the riches of the Triune
God, which are just His reality, possible and real in the Body of
Christ. All that the processed Triune God is, including righteousness, holiness, life, light, power, grace, and all the divine attributes, are realized by this Spirit of reality to be the real attributes
of the Body of Christ (Rom. 15:16b; 14:17; Eph. 3:16). Originally,
such righteousness, holiness, life, light, power, and grace were
merely God's attributes; now these attributes have been realized
in the church by the Spirit in the Body of Christ. The church
therefore possesses the reality of the divine attributes, such as
righteousness, holiness, life, light, power, and grace.

Furthermore, all that the Triune God experienced, including
incarnation, crucifixion, and resurrection, are likewise realized
by this Spirit of reality to be the real experiences of the Body of
Christ. Originally, it was the Triune God who was incarnated,

crucified, and resurrected. But when the Spirit of reality came, He made these experiences of the Triune God real in us as our real experiences. Because of this we can live a normal human life on the earth today. We can deal with the negative matters which befall us by the capacity of the death of Christ. We do not lose our temper, nor do we blame or rebuke others, because the death of Christ is realized in us through the Spirit of reality. Moreover, the Spirit with the resurrection of Christ works in us to enable us to love and forgive others. These are all examples of how the experiences of the Triune God Himself have been realized in the church by the Spirit of reality to be the real experiences of the church. This is the Spirit of the reality of the Triune God becoming the reality of the Body of Christ.

Finally, we need to see conclusively that both the essence and the reality of the Body of Christ are altogether matters of the Spirit of the processed and consummated Triune God. Whether essence or reality, it is all a matter of this Spirit. The Spirit is the reality of the essence as well as the essence to which the reality belongs. *Essence* emphasizes the inward substance, while *reality* emphasizes the outward realization. Because the Spirit is the inward substance of the Body of Christ, He is also its outward realization. Both the inward essence and substance and the outward reality and realization are of the Spirit. This Spirit is the secret to all that the Triune God is to the Body of Christ. For instance, the secret to God's loving the Body of Christ, sanctifying it, and strengthening it, is with the Spirit of reality. It is the Spirit of reality who makes God's love real in the Body of Christ, so that it may be sanctified and strengthened. This Spirit of reality is the processed Triune God Himself as well as the totality of all the attributes of the processed Triune God. If we have this Spirit, we have all the attributes of the processed Triune God, such as love, light, mercy, righteousness, holiness, life, power, and grace. (*A Thorough View of the Body of Christ,* pp. 31-33)

Further Reading: A Thorough View of the Body of Christ, chs. 1-2

Enlightenment and inspiration: _____

_____

_____

_____

Morning Nourishment

1 Cor. For even as the body is one and has many mem-
12:12 bers, yet all the members of the body, being many,
 are one body, so also is the Christ.
Eph. This mystery is great, but I speak with regard to
5:32 Christ and the church.

In the Bible *Christ* sometimes refers to the individual Christ, the personal Christ, and sometimes to the corporate Christ, to Christ and the church (1 Cor. 12:12)....Christ is the Head of this mysterious Christ, and the church is the Body of this mysterious Christ. The two have been joined together to become the one mysterious Christ, a universal great man. All the saved ones in all times and in all space added together become the Body of this mysterious Christ. Individually speaking, we, the saved ones, are particular members of the Body (1 Cor. 12:27). Corporately speaking, we are the mystical Body of Christ. Every saved one is a part of the Body of Christ. (*The Conclusion of the New Testament*, p. 2267)

Today's Reading

[In 1 Corinthians 12:12] Christ...is not the individual Christ but the corporate Christ, the Body-Christ. In Greek "Christ" in this verse is "the Christ," referring to the corporate Christ, composed of Christ Himself as the Head and the church as His Body with all the believers as its members. All the believers of Christ are organically united with Him and constituted of His life and element to become His Body, an organism, to express Him. Hence, He is not only the Head but also the Body. As our physical body has many members, yet is one, so is this Christ.

As a vine includes not only the stalk but also the branches, so the corporate Christ, the Body-Christ, includes not only Christ Himself but also the members of Christ's Body, who are the members of Christ, parts of Christ. According to our natural constitution, we cannot be members of Christ's Body. Christ Himself is the element, the factor, that makes us parts of Him. Therefore, in order to be parts of Christ, as members of His Body, we must have Christ wrought into our being.

In order to become the corporate Christ, the Body-Christ, Christ had to pass through the steps of a process. First He, the very God, became flesh for our redemption. Then in resurrection He became the life-giving Spirit to come into us and work within us. In this way He becomes the Body-Christ. Now in the church life we enjoy not only God, the Redeemer, and the life-giving Spirit but also the Christ who is the Body.

The church can be the Body of Christ only as the members are constituted of Christ, possessing His life and nature. If we consider our physical body, we shall realize that anything that does not have our life and nature cannot be part of our body. Just as our body is part of us, so Christ's Body, the church, is part of Him. As members of the Body, we are parts of Christ, constituted of Him.

Because the reality of Christ is the Spirit, the way to be constituted of Christ to be His Body is to drink the Spirit. The Body has been formed by the baptism in the one Spirit. In one Spirit we have all been baptized into one Body (1 Cor. 12:13). The baptism into the one Body has positioned us all to drink, and by drinking of the Spirit, we are constituted to be the Body. By drinking the Spirit, we experience the dispensing of the Divine Trinity into our being and are constituted to be the Body.

The building up of the Body of Christ is altogether a matter of constitution. The Body is an organic entity constituted of the divine element of the processed Triune God. It is through such a constitution that we become the Body of Christ. Therefore, what the Body of Christ needs is not organization but a unique constitution, a constitution which consists of the divine element wrought into our inner being through our drinking of the one Spirit. The more we drink the one Spirit, the more the divine element becomes our constituent to make us the one Body, the corporate Christ. (*The Conclusion of the New Testament,* pp. 2267-2269)

Further Reading: The Conclusion of the New Testament, msg. 212; *CWWL, 1973-1974,* vol. 1, "The Enjoyment of Christ for the Body in 1 Corinthians," chs. 3-4

Enlightenment and inspiration: _____

_____

_____

_____

Morning Nourishment

1 Cor. What then, brothers? Whenever you come together,
14:26 each one has a psalm, has a teaching, has a revelation, has a tongue, has an interpretation. Let all
things be done for building up.
Heb. Not abandoning our own assembling together, as the
10:25 custom with some is, but exhorting *one another*; and
so much the more as you see the day drawing near.

Many Christians today would say that they care only for
Christ and not for the church. If we care only for Christ and not
for the church, we can gain only a limited portion of Christ. We
can gain much more of the riches of Christ when we care for both
Christ and the church....We should pray, "Lord Jesus, I know
that today You are no longer only the individual Christ but also
the corporate Christ, the Head with the Body. You are the Body-
Christ. Therefore, Lord Jesus, I receive You as well as Your Body.
I receive the Body-Christ, and I desire to walk in this Christ."

Many of us in the Lord's recovery can testify that since the day
we came into the church and began to care for the church, there
has been a great difference in our spiritual life. We have the inner
sense that we are rich. Everyone in the church is a spiritual bil-
lionaire; we are all rich. (*CWWL, 1973-1974*, vol. 1, "The Vision
and Experience of the Corporate Christ," pp. 496-497)

Today's Reading

The Lord's word concerning the building up of the church as
the dwelling place of God and the Body of Christ must be fulfilled before His coming back. The Lord Jesus said in Matthew
24:35, "Heaven and earth will pass away, but My words shall by
no means pass away." Without the biblical way for us to meet
and to serve, the way that is illustrated, shown, and signified in
the New Testament, the Lord's words concerning the building
up of the church cannot be fulfilled. The traditional way to
meet and to serve surely cannot fulfill the Lord's words concerning the building up of His church.

If 1 Corinthians 14:26 and Hebrews 10:25 are not fulfilled,

there is no way for the building up of the house of God and of the Body of Christ. If we do not endeavor to take the scriptural way, this will delay the Lord's coming back. Heaven and earth will pass away at the time of the Lord's coming back, and His words will be fulfilled. Sooner or later verses like 1 Corinthians 14:26 and Hebrews 10:25 will be fulfilled. When Christians have a proper way to meet and to serve, that will afford the Lord the possibility to build up the church as the dwelling place of God and as the Body of Christ. I have the assurance that right now the Lord is doing something to bring His people back to the God-ordained way to meet and to serve that He may accomplish all He has prophesied and promised concerning the building up of His church.

Several points concerning the traditional way to meet and serve...include the following: the traditional way adopts the way of human society for religion—"in the customs of the nations" (2 Kings 17:8, NASB); the traditional way is natural, fitting man's natural and fallen condition; the traditional way does not require man to be living and in the spirit; and the traditional way is religious....We shall [also] consider some other points concerning the traditional way.

The traditional way of meeting accommodates the dead man's taste. Many of us who were in the traditional way in Christianity for a number of years can recall what we saw there. I attended Christianity services from my youth. I saw many people who were dead spiritually. The so-called church service just accommodated these dead people. Many of them were happy because they had a kind of social life, which they called the church. Week after week, Sunday after Sunday, a certain portion was read from the Bible as a subject, yet year-round there was no change in the people. They simply attended services every Sunday. (*CWWL, 1987,* vol. 3, "The Scriptural Way to Meet and to Serve for the Building Up of the Body of Christ," pp. 498-499, 319)

Further Reading: CWWL, 1973-1974, vol. 1, "The Vision and Experience of the Corporate Christ," chs. 3-4

Enlightenment and inspiration: _____

_____

_____

Morning Nourishment

2 Tim.   For which cause I remind you to fan into flame the
1:6-7   gift of God, which is in you through the laying on of
my hands. For God has not given us a spirit of cowardice, but of power and of love and of sober-
mindedness.

The scriptural way to meet and to serve surely is against the religious and social way of meeting and service....This way is spiritual. It fits the taste of the living and spiritual man and requires
man to be living and in the spirit. To take this way, we need to be re-
vived, to live a victorious life, and to walk by and according to the
spirit. For this way to be prevailing in our meeting and in our service, we also need to have an uninterrupted fellowship with the Lord
daily and hourly. We need to contact the Lord from the beginning of
each day by calling on His name and pray-reading His Word that
we may enjoy Him and be supplied with His riches. We need to
speak Him to people all day long whether in season or out of season. To live such a life for the scriptural way to meet and to serve
surely requires us always to pay a price....It is...against the religious life and social customs. For this we need to pray much and receive grace from the Lord. (*The Scriptural Way to Meet and to Serve
for the Building Up of the Body of Christ*, p. 328)

Today's Reading

The traditional way has bound and annulled the organic
function of the members of the Body of Christ for many centuries....Some would say that we need to have a meeting not only
to help the sinners get saved by preaching the gospel to them
but also to help the new ones get fed and edified. This sounds
very good, and everyone would say that this is needed, but the
subtlety of the evil one is present here.

The denominations have millions of members, but very few of
these members are useful. On the one hand, the clerical class, the
professionals, may help their so-called churches to be increased.
But on the other hand, they annul the function of the members
of the Body of Christ....With this kind of situation, where is the

possibility for the saints to be built up in an organic way—where their spirit has been regenerated, their soul is being transformed, and they are growing in spirit by the transformation in their soul together with other fellow members? Where are the saints experiencing the all-inclusive Christ and growing with Him, having the freedom and opportunity for their spiritual, organic function to be developed, and being built up together in the spirit so that not only a local church but also the whole Body of Christ can be built up as the full expression of God?

The traditional way has not only bound and annulled the spiritual function of the members of Christ but also has choked and even killed the living members of Christ for all the time in the past history of the church. On the one hand, the traditional way feeds people, but on the other hand, because of the clerical class, in many aspects it frustrates the believers from growing in life and even chokes them to death. Hence, most of the believers are spiritually dead in their church services. Although we have left organized Christianity, its traditional way to meet and to serve still influences us to quite an extent, and we are even under its bondage, without any awareness of its damage to the Body of Christ, which we are endeavoring to build up by all its members functioning in each one's measure (Eph. 4:16).

[In verse 16] *out from whom* means from Christ, the Head. *All the Body* includes all the members of the Body, not just the gifted ones. The *operation in the measure of each one part* means that each member has a measure for God's operation. *Each one part* refers to every member of the Body. Every member of the Body of Christ has its own measure, which works for the growth of the Body. In the traditional way, can we see the building up of the Body of Christ mentioned in verse 12 or particularly in verse 16? (*CWWL, 1987,* vol. 3, "The Scriptural Way to Meet and to Serve for the Building Up of the Body of Christ," pp. 321-323)

Further Reading: CWWL, 1987, vol. 3, "The Scriptural Way to Meet and to Serve for the Building Up of the Body of Christ," chs. 1-5

Enlightenment and inspiration: _____

_____

_____

_____

Morning Nourishment

Eph. But holding to truth in love, we may grow up into
4:15-16 Him in all things, who is the Head, Christ, out from
whom all the Body, being joined together and
being knit together through every joint of the rich
supply and *through* the operation in the measure
of each one part, causes the growth of the Body
unto the building up of itself in love.

The scriptural way to meet and to serve is able to develop the
organic function and ability of the members of Christ and is able
to build up the Body of Christ (Eph. 4:12, 16). Ephesians 4:12 tells
us that the gifted persons do their work to perfect the saints that
the saints may carry out the work of the ministry for the building
up of the Body of Christ. Verse 16 follows to tell us in detail how
the perfected saints build up the Body directly.... *Every joint of the
rich supply* refers to the specially gifted persons, and *each one
part* refers to every member of the Body. After we are perfected by
the gifted persons, we have to function. One who is a joint, a gifted
person, has to render the supply to the Body. Furthermore, as
long as you are one part among the many parts of the Body of
Christ, you also have a measure of ability, a measure of function.
(*CWWL, 1987,* vol. 3, "The Scriptural Way to Meet and to Serve for
the Building Up of the Body of Christ," pp. 342-343)

Today's Reading

The building up of the Body must be organic. It is altogether
a matter of life. Without life, there is no genuine building up of
the church. There is very little of the element of life in today's
Christianity. What we see built up among most of today's
Christians is mostly inorganic. According to the New Testament, however, the building up of the church should be altogether in life. The Body of Christ is like our physical body. In
our physical body no part is lifeless.

The organic building up of the Body of Christ is the increase of
the Triune God in the believers for their growth in Christ.... [In
Colossians 2:19] *grows with the growth of God* may also be

translated "grows with the increase of God." God is increasing in us in essence essentially. It is by this essential increase of God in us that the church as the Body of Christ grows. The church as the Body of Christ grows with some element, with some essence. A person grows with the essence of the food that he takes in. (*CWWL, 1989*, vol. 4, "The Advance of the Lord's Recovery Today," pp. 61, 41)

The Lord desires to recover the church meetings in mutuality with all speaking for building up (1 Cor. 14:23a, 26, 31). (*Prophesying in the Church Meetings for the Organic Building Up of the Church as the Body of Christ (Outlines)*, p. 10)

God's administration is a family matter. In ancient times the administration among large families was mainly for distributing the food, the necessities, to all the members of the family. Our God has the biggest family in the universe. God has a family plan to distribute all His rich provision to His children. His rich provision is altogether embodied in a person, the second of the Trinity, Christ. All the riches of the Godhead and the fullness of the Godhead are embodied in Christ. God's family plan, God's family administration, is to distribute, to dispense, all the divine riches in Christ into His saved ones for their nourishment and feeding, resulting in the building up of the Body of Christ. Today we are under God's economy to enjoy His rich distribution.

We are now under God's dispensing, and this dispensing is by prophesying. Prophesying is the unique way, the best way, the excelling way, to dispense all the riches of Christ into God's people for the building up of the organic Body of Christ. The dispensing of the riches of Christ by prophesying can be illustrated by the dispensing of food by a mother. Day by day a mother distributes, or dispenses, food to her little baby until he becomes a strong and husky boy....To prophesy is to distribute, to dispense, the Triune God as the rich food, the nourishing element, into others. (*CWWL, 1988*, vol. 4, "The Present Advance of the Lord's Recovery," p. 571)

Further Reading: The Scriptural Way to Meet and to Serve for the Building Up of the Body of Christ, chs. 6-8, 16-17

Enlightenment and inspiration: _____

_____

_____

_____

Hymns, #1225

1   Lord, to know Thee as the Body,
    Is my desperate need today,
    Oh, to see Thee in Thy members,
    'Tis for this I long and pray.
    No more just to know Thy headship,
    In an individual way,
    But to see Thee incarnated,
    As the Body-Christ, I pray.

2   Through the years, Thy saints
        have sought Thee,
    Longing for reality;
    Gazing upward, searching inward,
    Thirsting for the sight of Thee.
    Now reveal that Christ in heaven
    Is the Body manifest;
    And the Christ who dwells within us
    As the Body is expressed.

3   Prone to be misled, I know it,
    By my lofty thoughts of Thee;
    Easy 'tis for self to seek Thee,
    Yet not touch reality.
    Oh, how much I need to find Thee,
    In Thy members here below.
    God eternal dwells among us,
    Manifest in flesh to know.

4   Limit, Lord, my independence,
    Let me to Thy Body turn;
    Not just seeking light from heaven,
    But the church's sense to learn.
    May we be the stones for building,
    Not the formless, useless clay;
    Gain in us Thy heart's desire,
    Corporately Thyself display.

Composition for prophecy with main point and sub-points: _____

The Status of the Church—the New Man

Scripture Reading: Eph. 2:15-16; 4:22-24; Col. 3:10-11

Day 1   I. **The church, the Body of Christ, is the one new man to accomplish God's eternal purpose (Eph. 1:9, 11; 3:11; 2:15-16; 4:22-24; Rom. 8:28; 2 Tim. 1:9):**

A. God's intention in His creation of man was to have a corporate man to express Him and to represent Him (Gen. 1:26).

B. God's creation of man in Genesis 1 is a picture of the new man in God's new creation; this means that the old creation is a figure, a type, of the new creation (Eph. 2:15; 4:24; 2 Cor. 5:17).

C. Eventually, the church as the one new man is the corporate man in God's intention; the one new man fulfills the twofold purpose of expressing God and dealing with God's enemy (Gen. 1:26).

II. **The one new man was created through Christ's death on the cross (Eph. 2:15-16):**

A. The one new man was created by Christ with two kinds of material—the redeemed created man and the divine element; on the cross Christ put these two materials together to produce a new man.

B. In the creating of the new man, first our natural man was crucified by Christ, and then through the crossing out of the old man, Christ imparted the divine element into us, causing us to become a new entity (Rom. 6:6; 2 Cor. 5:17).

Day 2   C. Apart from being in Christ, we could not have been created into one new man, because in ourselves we do not have the divine essence, which is the element of the new man (Eph. 2:15):

1. Only in the divine essence and with the divine essence were we created into the one new man; it is possible to have this essence only in Christ.

2. Christ Himself is the essence of the new man; hence, in Himself He created the two, the Jews and the Gentiles, into one new man.

3. In the one new man Christ is all because He is the essence with which the new man was created; therefore, the one new man is Christ (Col. 3:11).

III. **The church is the one new man, and in this new man Christ is all and in all; we have no place (vv. 10-11):**

A. God's intention in His economy is that Christ be everything; therefore, it is crucial for us to see that God wants nothing but Christ and that in the eyes of God nothing counts except Christ (Matt. 17:5; Col. 1:18; 2:2, 17; 3:4, 10-11):

Day 3
1. God's intention is to make Christ His Son the center of His economy and also to make Him everything to the believers (1:18; 2:17).

2. God's economy is to work the all-inclusive Christ into us (Gal. 4:19; Eph. 3:17a; Col. 3:11).

B. There is no natural person in the one new man, and there is no possibility, no room, for any natural person (vv. 10-11):

1. In the one new man there is only one person—the all-inclusive Christ (2:17; 3:4, 11).

2. The one new man is just Christ—Christ spreading and Christ enlarged.

C. The new man is uniquely one—one in Christ and one with Christ; we are one by Christ and through Christ (Eph. 2:15; Col. 3:11):

1. If we are not in Christ, we have no share, no part, in the new man; rather, we are through with the new man.

2. If we are in Christ but do not live Christ, we have a problem related to the new man.

Day 4
D. The one new man comes into being as we are saturated, filled, and permeated with Christ and replaced by Him through an organic process (2 Cor. 3:18):

1. The new man is Christ in all the saints permeating us and replacing us until all natural distinctions have been removed and everyone is constituted of Christ (Col. 3:11).
2. The all-inclusive Christ must be wrought into us organically until He replaces our natural being with Himself (Eph. 3:17a; Gal. 4:19).

E. In the one new man, Christ is all the members and is in all the members (Col. 3:11):
1. The Christ who dwells in us is the constituent of the one new man (1:27; 3:11).
2. Because Christ is all the members of the new man, there is no room in the new man for any race, nationality, culture, or social status (vv. 10-11).
3. In order for us to experience the reality of Christ being all the members of the new man, we need to take Christ as our life and person and live Him, not ourselves (Gal. 2:20; Phil. 1:20-21a).

Day 5
4. It is very significant that Paul said both that Christ is all and that He is in all (Col. 3:11):
   a. We should not think that because Christ is all the members of the one new man, we are nothing and are not needed.
   b. The fact that Christ is in all the members of the new man indicates that the members continue to exist (v. 11).

IV. **We need to see that all the local churches in the different countries are one new man (vv. 10-11; 4:15-16):**
A. All the churches are not merely individual local churches but are the one new man (Eph. 2:15-16):
1. We cannot say that each local church is a new man; rather, all the local churches on earth are the one new man (4:24).
2. The one new man is a matter not merely of individual localities and individual churches

but of all the churches on earth corporately.

B. Among the churches in the Lord's recovery, there should be no "nations" (Matt. 16:18; 1 Thes. 1:1; Rom. 16:16b; 3 John 9-10):

1. We do not care to have a little "nation," an empire, in which we can be a king; rather, we care to be in the one new man (Matt. 20:25-26a).

2. The building of the church depends on the existence of the one new man (16:18; Eph. 2:21-22).

Day 6   C. Today is the day to have a new man constituted of all the local churches, including all the saints as one in Christ, who is all in all; this will be the ultimate church life—a universal new man living out Christ (Col. 3:10-11; Eph. 4:24; Phil. 1:20-21a).

V. **The goal of the Lord's recovery is to bring forth the one new man (Eph. 2:15; 4:22-24; Col. 3:10-11):**

A. What was divided and scattered in the old man is recovered in the new man; to put off the old man is to put off the divided and scattered man; to put on the new man is to put on the gathered and one new man (Gen. 11:5-9; Acts 2:5-12; Eph. 4:22, 24; Col. 3:10-11).

B. What the Lord has been doing and is now doing in His recovery is bringing forth the one new man with Himself as the life and the person for God's expression (Eph. 3:17-19; Col. 3:4, 10-11).

C. The requirement that everyone be only one man is exceedingly high; for the practical existence of the one new man, we need to rise up together to take Christ as our person (Gal. 2:20; Eph. 2:15; 3:17a).

D. The one new man will conclude this age, usher in the kingdom of God, and bring Christ, the King, back to this earth (Rev. 11:15).

Morning Nourishment

Eph.   Abolishing in His flesh the law of the command-
2:15-16   ments in ordinances, that He might create the two
in Himself into one new man, *so* making peace, and
might reconcile both in one Body to God through
the cross, having slain the enmity by it.

God did not create many men; He created mankind collectively in one person, Adam. God created such a corporate man
in His image and according to His likeness so that mankind
might express God corporately. (Gen. 1:26, footnote 4)

God created a corporate man not only to express Himself
with His image but also to represent Him by exercising His
dominion over all things. (Gen. 1:26, footnote 5)

Today's Reading

God's creation of man in Genesis 1 is a picture of the new
man in God's new creation. This means that the old creation is a
figure, a type, of the new creation....In both the old creation and
the new creation man is the center.

God created man in His own image (Gen. 1:26) and then
gave man His dominion. Image is for expression. God wants
man to be His expression....God [also] wants man to represent
Him in His authority for His dominion. In the old creation man
was created to have God's image to express Him and also to
have His dominion to represent Him.

God's positive intention is that man would express Him,
whereas God's negative intention is that man would deal with
God's enemy, Satan, the devil. In the universe God has a problem, the problem of dealing with His enemy. Since God's enemy,
the devil, is a creature, God will not deal with him directly Himself; instead, He will deal with him by man, a creature of His creation. God deals with His enemy through man.

In the old creation the dominion given to man was limited to
the earth. This means that in the old creation the dealing with
God's enemy was restricted to the earth. However, in God's new
creation the dominion has been enlarged to the entire universe.

Eventually, the church as the new man is the man in God's intention. God wanted a man, and in the old creation He created a figure, a type, not the real man. The real man is the man Christ created on the cross through His all-inclusive death. This man is called the new man.

The term *the new man* reminds us of the old man. The old man did not fulfill God's dual purpose. However, the new man in God's new creation does fulfill the twofold purpose of expressing God and dealing with God's enemy. (*The Conclusion of the New Testament,* pp. 2302-2303)

Thousands of Christians have read Ephesians 2:15; 4:24; and Colossians 3:10, and they have seen the term *the new man* according to the letter, but they do not know what the new man is. Our becoming the new man was not merely a matter of our repenting and being sorry for our past and thereby becoming new. This is the teaching of Confucius; it is not the teaching of the Bible. In the creating of the new man, first our natural man was crucified by Christ on the cross, and then through the crossing out of the old man, Christ imparted God's element into us. Thus, we became an entity that is different from the old man, because we have God's element in us.

Ephesians 2:15 tells us that Christ did this creating work on the cross. We usually consider that Christ's work on the cross was related only to negative things, to cross us out, to crucify us. But Ephesians 2:15 tells us that on the cross Christ did something positive, to generate us, not to put us to death. This divine thought is clearly seen in Ephesians 2:15. The cross of Christ not only destroys and kills; it also generates and brings in something divine.

The new man was created by Christ with two kinds of materials. The first is the redeemed created man; the second is the divine element. On the cross Christ put these two materials together to produce a new man. (*The God-men,* p. 17)

Further Reading: The Conclusion of the New Testament, msgs.
  216-217

Enlightenment and inspiration: _____

_____

_____

Morning Nourishment

Matt.   While he was still speaking, behold, a bright cloud
17:5   overshadowed them, and behold, a voice out of the
        cloud, saying, This is My Son, the Beloved, in
        whom I have found My delight. Hear Him!
Col.   And He is the Head of the Body, the church; He is
1:18   the beginning, the Firstborn from the dead, that
        He Himself might have the first place in all things.

Since death ushers us into resurrection, in His resurrection Christ put us into Himself. Then with His divine essence He created us in Himself into the one new man.

[In Ephesians 2:15] do not ignore the phrase "in Himself." Apart from being in Him, we could not have been created into the new man, because in ourselves we do not have the divine essence, which is the element of the new man....It is possible to have this essence only in Christ. In fact, Christ Himself is this essence, this element. Hence, in Himself Christ created the two into one new man. We all need to be profoundly impressed with the fact that we, the believers, have been created into one new man in Christ. (*Life-study of Ephesians*, pp. 211-212)

Today's Reading

In the one new man there are none of the national and cultural distinctions between the peoples. Here there is neither Jew nor Gentile, bondman nor freeman, cultured nor uncultured (Col. 3:10-11). Likewise, there is no American, nor British, nor Japanese, nor Chinese, nor German, nor French. In this new man Christ is all because He is the very essence with which the new man is created. Hence, the new man is just Christ.

Because the new man has been created in Christ and with Christ according to God, the new man bears the image of God. In contrast to Genesis 1:26, which says that man was made in the image of God, Ephesians 4:24 says that the new man is created directly according to God. Eventually, the new man will bear the image of God in holiness and righteousness of the reality. By being renewed in the governing spirit of our mind, we put on this new man that has been created in Christ Jesus. (*Life-study of Ephesians,* pp. 214-215)

The church should be a house filled with Christ and constituted with Him. Instead, the church [in Colossae] had been invaded by culture. To a large extent, Christ as the unique element in the church life was being replaced by various aspects of this mixed culture. The constituent of the church should be Christ and Christ alone, for the church is the Body of Christ....Nevertheless, the good elements of culture, especially philosophy and religion, had invaded the church and saturated it....We must see that Satan's strategy in flooding the church with culture is to use the most highly developed aspects of culture to replace Christ.

Therefore, Paul's purpose in the book of Colossians is to show that in the church nothing should be allowed to be a substitute for Christ. The church life must be constituted uniquely of Christ.... This is the reason that in this short Epistle a number of elevated expressions are used to describe Christ. For example, He is called the image of the invisible God, the Firstborn of all creation, the Firstborn from among the dead, and the body of all the shadows. In 3:10 and 11, Paul says that in the new man there is no possibility of having Greek or Jew, circumcision or uncircumcision, barbarian or Scythian, slave or freeman. Rather, in the new man Christ is all and in all. This means that Christ must be everyone and in everyone....Christ must be every one of us. In the new man Christ must be you and me. Not only must culture go, but even we have to go. It is crucial that we see this revelation.

The main point in the Epistle of Colossians is the fact that in the eyes of God nothing counts except Christ. This fact excludes both good things and bad things, both sinful things and cultured things....The book of Colossians teaches us that in the church life Christ must be all and in all. Everything that is not Christ must go. (*Life-study of Colossians,* pp. 2-3, 5-7)

Further Reading: Life-study of Ephesians, msg. 24; *The Conclusion of the New Testament,* msg. 218

Enlightenment and inspiration: _____

_____

_____

Morning Nourishment

Col. Which are a shadow of the things to come, but the
2:17 body is of Christ.
Gal. My children, with whom I travail again in birth
4:19 until Christ is formed in you.

Paul in 1 Corinthians 1:1-9 impresses us with the fact that
in God's economy, Christ is the unique center. God's intention is
to make Christ His Son the center of His economy and also to
make Him everything to all the believers. For this reason Paul
tells us that Christ is both theirs and ours and that we have
been called into the fellowship of the Son, Jesus Christ our
Lord. In His economy God's intention is to make Christ everything, to give Christ to us as our portion, and to work Christ
into us. (*The Conclusion of the New Testament*, p. 3118)

Today's Reading

God's economy is to work a wonderful person into our being.
This person is the all-inclusive Christ, the One who is the reality of every positive thing in the universe. Christ is the Firstborn of all creation. He is both God and man, for the One who
was the eternal God became incarnated at a point in time.
Hence, Christ is the real God and the real man. He possesses
all the divine attributes and human virtues. He is the reality of
love, life, light, grace, humility, patience, power, mercy, wisdom,
righteousness, and holiness. (*Life-study of Colossians*, p. 313)

Not only is there no natural person in the new man, but
there is no possibility and no room for any natural person to
exist. (Col. 3:11, footnote 2)

This, however, does not mean that He is in you as your
person, He is in me as my person, and He is in another one as
his person. This is an improper understanding. I tell you that
He is in all of us as one person. The person in you is the person
who is in me. We all have only one person. Who is this person?
This person is Christ. (*CWWL, 1977*, vol. 3, "One Body, One
Spirit, and One New Man," p. 314)

The new man is not a new organization or a new "United

Nations." This new man is just Christ—Christ spreading and Christ enlarged. Colossians 3:11 says, "Where there cannot be Greek and Jew, circumcision and uncircumcision, barbarian, Scythian, slave, free man, but Christ is all and in all." All persons have no place in the new man; it is not another kind of United Nations. You have no place in the new man, and neither do I. We all have no place in the new man, but Christ is all and in all.

The new man is not ecumenical. The new man is uniquely one, one with Christ and one in Christ. No one has any place in the new man, neither Jew, Greek, circumcision, uncircumcision, barbarian, Scythian, slave nor free man, but Christ is all and in all. We are not an ecumenical movement; we are in the new man. We are one not by our niceness, gentleness, or humility but by and through Christ, because Christ is in you and Christ is in me. Christ is in all the brothers from China and all the brothers from Japan. We all have Christ, and Christ is our oneness. What we have is not a unity or an ecumenical movement. What we have is simply Christ. This does not mean that you tolerate me and I tolerate you but that you have Christ and I have Christ. I love Him and you love Him; you live by Him and I live by Him. We all have Christ, so we are one in the unique Christ. If we do not have Christ and live Christ, we are through with the new man. The Lord's recovery is not a movement. It is altogether the life of Christ, Christ as our life and our person. We all have to see this in a crystal clear way.

If you are not in Christ, you are through with this new man. If you are not in Christ, you have no share, no part, in this new man. Even if you are in Christ, yet you do not live by Christ, you have a problem related to this new man....We are here living Christ. Even if you are a typical Chinese, what is in you now is not Chinese; rather Christ is in you. Christ is our life, Christ is our nature, and Christ is our person. (*CWWL, 1977,* vol. 3, "The One New Man," pp. 489-491, 490)

Further Reading: CWWL, 1977, vol. 3, "One Body, One Spirit, and One New Man," ch. 5; "The One New Man," ch. 3

Enlightenment and inspiration: _____

_____

_____

_____

Morning Nourishment

Col. And have put on the new man, which is being re-
3:10-11 newed unto full knowledge according to the image
of Him who created him, where there cannot be
Greek and Jew, circumcision and uncircumcision,
barbarian, Scythian, slave, free man, but Christ is
all and in all.

In the new man Christ is all. In the church as the new man,
Christ is everything. This implies that He is every brother and
every sister. This also implies that every brother and sister
must be constituted of Christ. In the new man there cannot
be Jewish members and Gentile members; there can only be
Christ-members. If we would be constituted of Christ, Christ
must be added into us more and more. We must be permeated
with Christ, saturated with Christ, and have Christ organically wrought into our being. Eventually, we shall be replaced
by Christ. Then, in reality, He will be all and in all. He will be
every member, every part, of the new man.

The new man does not come into existence by taking Christians from various countries and bringing them together. That
would be a new organization, not the new man. The new man
comes into being as we are saturated, filled, and permeated with
Christ and replaced by Him through an organic process. The new
man is Christ in all the saints permeating us and replacing us
until all natural distinctions have been eliminated and everyone
is constituted of Christ. (*Life-study of Colossians,* pp. 454-455)

Today's Reading

Christ as all and in all in the new man should not be mere
doctrine. Rather, the rich, substantial Christ must actually be
wrought into us organically until He replaces our natural
being with Himself. This can take place only as we remain
rooted in Him and absorb His riches into us. These riches will
then become the substance, the element, which will saturate us
organically. Then Christ will become us, and we shall become
constituted of Christ. This is not only to grow with Christ, but it

is also to be built up in Christ.

In Colossians 3:11 Paul says not only that Christ is all, but also that He is in all. In other words, on the one hand, Christ is all the members, and on the other hand, He is in all the members.

In the new man Christ is every member. Concerning this, Paul says in 3:11, "Where there cannot be Greek and Jew, circumcision and uncircumcision, barbarian, Scythian, slave, freeman, but Christ is all and in all." This means that in the new man there is no place, no room, for any natural person. There is no place for regional, cultural, or national distinctions. For example, in the new man there cannot be Chinese or Americans, Californians or Texans. Likewise, in the new man there is no room for Jew or Greek, for religious ones or nonreligious ones, for cultured ones or uncultured ones, for freemen or slaves. There is no room for any race, nationality, culture, or social status. In the one new man there is room only for Christ. Christ surely is all the members of the new man. (*Life-study of Colossians*, pp. 455, 537, 536)

In Colossians 3:11 Paul says not only that in the new man there is no room for any natural person but that in the new man "Christ is all and in all." In the new man there is room only for Christ. He is all the members of the new man, and He is in all the members. He is everything in the new man. This means that actually He is the new man.

For us to experience the reality of Christ being all the members of the new man, we need to take Christ as our life and person and live Him, not ourselves. If Christ is the living of all the saints, all the members of the new man, then in reality only He will be in the new man. When all the saints, whatever their nationality may be, live Christ, then in a real and practical way Christ will be all the members of the new man. (*The Conclusion of the New Testament*, p. 2315)

Further Reading: Life-study of Colossians, msgs. 28, 60

Enlightenment and inspiration: _____

_____

_____

_____

Morning Nourishment

Col.   Greet the brothers in Laodicea, as well as Nym-
4:15-16 phas and the church, which is in his house. And
         when this letter is read among you, cause that it be
         read in the church of the Laodiceans also, and that
         you also read the one from Laodicea.

Since Paul says that Christ is all, why is there the need for
him to say that Christ is in all? If Paul did not say that Christ is
in all, only that He is all, then we may think that in the new
man Christ is needed and that we are not needed. We should
not think that, because Christ is all the members in the new
man, we are nothing and are not needed. On the one hand, the
Bible does say that in the new man there is no place for the natural person because Christ is all the members. Yet, on the other
hand, Paul says that Christ is in the members. The fact that
Christ is in the members of the new man indicates that the
members still exist. (*Life-study of Colossians*, p. 537)

Today's Reading

When we take Christ as our life and live together with Him,
seeking the things which are above, we have the sense deep
within that we are one with Christ and that Christ is us. But
simultaneously we have an even deeper sense that Christ is in
us. Therefore, it is true to say that Christ is both in us and that
He is us. We are part of the new man with Christ in us. We continue to exist, but we do not exist without Christ; we are those
indwelt by Christ. (*Life-study of Colossians*, p. 537)

If we have all seen the vision of the new man and have seen
that all the churches are not merely individual local churches but
the one new man, we will be willing to say, "Lord, I want to receive
grace and mercy with all the saints as the one new man, taking
You as the person in all of us." If you take Christ in this way as the
person of this corporate new man, you will not decide anything in
your life by yourself. Because you see that you are a part of the
churches as the new man, you will not be able to decide anything
merely by yourself. Since you are a part of the new man, your

decisions and your living should not be yours; they should be the decisions and the living of the corporate new man.

We say that we are in the Lord's recovery, but if the Lord were to come among us, would He find this new man? This is not merely a matter of individual localities and individual churches; it involves all the churches on earth corporately. Are all the local churches on the earth in the Lord's recovery today truly the one new man? Because the church is a lampstand, you may say that each locality is a lampstand. However, concerning the church being the new man, can you say that each locality is a new man? No, you cannot. All the churches on the earth are the one new man. (*CWWL, 1977,* vol. 3, "One Body, One Spirit, and One New Man," pp. 321-322)

We should not desire to be a leader, and we should not desire to have a "nation." This is a great snare in Christianity. Every Christian denomination is a "nation." Even every free group is a nation, an empire. In this situation there could never be the oneness. In the Lord's recovery, among all the local churches, there should be no "nations." On the whole earth all the local churches are not "nations" but one new man. If we have many "nations," spontaneously there will be organization. But if we do not have such nations, we will be simply, singly, and uniquely the one new man.

The Lord prophesied in Matthew 16:18 that He would build His church. Whatever the Lord has prophesied must be fulfilled. Without the practical existence of the new man, the building up of the church may be vain talk. The building of the church depends upon the existence of the new man. If the new man comes into existence, no doubt, the builded church is here. Regardless of the present situation of division, the Lord is going to get the new man. Everything that the Lord is doing in this present age is to usher in the practical existence of the one new man. (*CWWL, 1977,* vol. 3, "The One New Man," pp. 497-498, 520)

Further Reading: Life-study of Colossians, msg. 31; *CWWL, 1977,* vol. 3, "One Body, One Spirit, and One New Man," ch. 6; "The One New Man," ch. 4

Enlightenment and inspiration: _____
_____
_____
_____

Morning Nourishment

Eph. And *that* you be renewed in the spirit of your mind.
4:23
Rev. And the seventh angel trumpeted; and there were
11:15 loud voices in heaven, saying, The kingdom of the
world has become the *kingdom* of our Lord and of
His Christ, and He will reign forever and ever.

When the new man is brought into full existence, we will not speak of the differences between the churches or of the jurisdiction and autonomy of the local churches. At that time we will all be living Christ. Only Christ will be among us, and only Christ will be manifested. (*CWWL, 1977,* vol. 3, "The One New Man," p. 492)

Today's Reading

If you go to Brazil, you will see Christ. If you go to Britain, you will see Christ. If you go to Italy, France, Japan, China, Korea, or the Philippines, you will see nothing but Christ. There will be no need to say that we all are one—Christ will be each one of us. Christ is with you, Christ is with me, Christ is with every believer, and Christ is with every local church. There will be no need to merely speak about oneness. We will simply live out Christ. This will be the ultimate church life, a universal new man living out Christ. This will conclude this age, usher in the kingdom, and bring Christ back. Eventually, this new man will become the loving bride to Christ.... All the saints in many countries throughout the world will speak the same thing (1 Cor. 1:10), the unique Christ. We will only speak Christ because we will be living Him out. He is our life, and He is our person. He is the life-giving Spirit within our spirit, and all the time, in everything, we are turning to our spirit and growing into this unique Christ.

What is here in the Lord's recovery is nothing but Christ, and this Christ is all and in all. You cannot be an individual believer, and you cannot keep your local church separate from all the others. Today is the day to have a new man constituted with all the local churches, including all the saints as one in Christ, who is all and in all. This vision will rescue us from all things other than Christ.

The church was brought forth not just with one people but with many peoples. In Acts 2:9-11 at least fifteen nationalities speaking at least fifteen dialects were represented. Although all these were Jews (v. 5), under God's sovereignty all these Jews were not of one language. They were people of many different dialects. They were Jews, but they were divided and scattered. However, when the time came for the church to be brought forth, they were all gathered together, and in that gathering, the church was produced. This indicates that what was divided and scattered in the old man was fully recovered in the new man. In the old man, man was divided and scattered, but in the new man, man is gathered and made one.

To put off the old man is to put off the divided and scattered man. To put on the new man (Eph. 4:24) is to put on the gathered and one new man, "which was created according to God in righteousness and holiness of the reality" (v. 24). (*CWWL, 1977*, vol. 3, "The One New Man," pp. 492-493, 477)

The Lord today is doing this work on the earth, and this is the goal of the Lord's recovery today. All those who love Him, pursue Him, and follow Him on the entire earth today must be renewed in the spirit of their mind to become the one new man, taking Him as their person and living by Him. This is what the Lord wants today.

The requirement that is high enough is that we would be for the universal new man. We need to take the Lord Jesus as our person; this includes everything, such as dealing with our sins, consecration, and seeking the will of God.

We truly need message after message to unveil every one of us so that we can see that today in the Lord's recovery we need to become the universal new man, and that we all need to rise up together to take Christ as our person. (*CWWL, 1977*, vol. 3, "One Body, One Spirit, and One New Man," pp. 350, 324)

Further Reading: Life-study of Colossians, msg. 62; *One Body, One Spirit, and One New Man,* ch. 7; *The One New Man,* ch. 6

Enlightenment and inspiration: _____

_____

_____

_____

Hymns, #1230

1 One new man is the Father's plan;
   He redeemed us from the sons of men.
   Every kindred, tribe and tongue,
   In Himself He called us to be one.
   God's expression on the earth
   Now reveals His glorious worth.
   One new man is the Father's plan;
   He redeemed us from the sons of men.

2 On the cross ordinances slain,
   That He might form just one of twain.
   Reconciling us to God,
   Thus on the serpent's head He trod.
   He breaks down the middle wall
   As upon His name we call;
   On the cross ordinances slain,
   That He might form just one of twain.

3 For this cause Your Person, Lord,
   We take and stand in one accord;
   All the members self forsake,
   And of the Body-Christ partake.
   We in Christ as one new man
   Now come forth to take this land.
   For this cause Your person, Lord,
   We take and stand in one accord.

Composition for prophecy with main point and sub-points: _____

_____
_____
_____
_____
_____
_____
_____
_____
_____
_____
_____
_____
_____
_____
_____
_____
_____
_____
_____
_____
_____
_____
_____
_____
_____
_____
_____
_____
_____
_____
_____
_____
_____

The Status of the Church—
the Counterpart of Christ

Scripture Reading: Gen. 2:18-25; John 19:34; Eph. 5:25-27, 32

Day 1   I. **The entire Bible is a divine romance, a record of how God courts His chosen people and eventually marries them (Gen. 2:21-24; S. S. 1:2-4; Isa. 54:5; 62:5; Jer. 2:2; 3:1, 14; 31:32; Ezek. 16:8; 23:5; Hosea 2:7, 19; Matt. 9:15; John 3:29; 2 Cor. 11:2; Eph. 5:25-32; Rev. 19:7; 21:2, 9-10; 22:17):**

   A. When we as God's people enter into a love relationship with God, we receive His life, just as Eve received the life of Adam (Gen. 2:21-22).

   B. It is this life that enables us to become one with God and makes Him one with us.

   C. In order for God and His people to be one, there must be a mutual love between them (John 14:21, 23; Exo. 20:6).

   D. The love between God and His people unfolded in the Bible is primarily like the affectionate love between a man and a woman (Jer. 2:2; 31:3).

   E. As God's people love God and spend time to fellowship with Him in His word, God infuses them with His divine element, making them one with Him as His spouse, the same as He is in life, nature, and expression (Psa. 119:140, 15-16; Eph. 5:25-27).

Day 2 II. **In Genesis 2 we see a picture of Christ and the church in the types of Adam and Eve:**

   A. Adam typifies God in Christ as the real, universal Husband, who is seeking a wife for Himself (Rom. 5:14; cf. Isa. 54:5; John 3:29; 2 Cor. 11:2; Eph. 5:31-32; Rev. 21:9).

   B. "Jehovah God said, It is not good for the man to be alone; I will make him a helper as his counterpart" (Gen. 2:18):

   1. Adam's need for a wife typifies and portrays

God's need, in His economy, to have a wife as His counterpart, His complement (lit., His parallel).

2. Although God, Christ, is absolutely and eternally perfect, He is not complete without the church as His wife.

3. God desires to have both Adam, typifying Christ, and Eve, typifying the church; His purpose is to "let them have dominion" (1:26); His purpose is to have a victorious Christ plus a victorious church, a Christ who has overcome the work of the devil plus a church that has overthrown the work of the devil; God wants Christ and the church to have dominion (Rom. 5:17; 16:20; Eph. 1:22-23).

Day 3 III. **We need to see what God did in order to produce a counterpart for Himself:**

A. From the ground God formed every animal of the field and every bird of heaven and brought them to Adam, "and the man gave names to all cattle and to the birds of heaven and to every animal of the field, but for Adam there was not found a helper as his counterpart" (Gen. 2:19-20):

1. The wife must be the same as the husband in life, nature, and expression.

2. Among the cattle, the birds, and the animals, Adam did not find a counterpart for himself, one that could match him.

B. In order to produce a counterpart for Himself, God first became a man, as typified by God's creation of Adam (John 1:14; Rom. 5:14).

C. "Jehovah God caused a deep sleep to fall upon the man, and he slept; and He took one of his ribs and closed up the flesh in its place" (Gen. 2:21):

1. Adam's deep sleep for the producing of Eve as his wife typifies Christ's death on the cross for the producing of the church as His counterpart (Eph. 5:25-27).

Day 4

    2. In the Bible sleep often refers to death (1 Cor. 15:18; 1 Thes. 4:13-16; John 11:11-14).

    3. Christ's death is the life-releasing, life-imparting, life-propagating, life-multiplying, life-reproducing death, which is signified by the grain of wheat falling into the ground to die and to grow up in order to produce many grains (12:24) for the making of the loaf, which is the Body, the church (1 Cor. 10:17).

    4. Through Christ's death the divine life within Him was released, and through His resurrection His released divine life was imparted into His believers for the constituting of the church.

    5. Through such a process God in Christ has been wrought into man with His life and nature so that man can be the same as God in life and nature in order to match Him as His counterpart.

  D. "Jehovah God built the rib, which He had taken from the man, into a woman and brought her to the man" (Gen. 2:22):

    1. The rib taken from Adam's opened side typifies the unbreakable, indestructible eternal life of Christ (Heb. 7:16; John 19:32-33, 36; Exo. 12:46; Psa. 34:20), which flowed out of His pierced side (John 19:34) to impart life to His believers for the producing and building up of the church as His counterpart:

Day 5

      a. Out of Christ's side came blood and water, but all that came out of Adam's side was the rib without the blood.

      b. At Adam's time there was no need of redemption through the blood, because there was no sin.

      c. However, by the time that Christ was "sleeping" on the cross, there was the problem of sin; thus, the blood that came out of Christ's side was for our judicial redemption.

   d. Following the blood, the water came out, which is the flowing life of God for our organic salvation (Exo. 17:6; 1 Cor. 10:4; Num. 20:8); this divine, flowing, uncreated life is typified by the rib taken out of Adam's side (Rom. 5:10).

2. Genesis 2:22 does not say that Eve was created but that she was built; the building of Eve with the rib taken from Adam's side typifies the building of the church with the resurrection life released from Christ through His death on the cross and imparted into His believers in His resurrection (John 12:24; 1 Pet. 1:3).

3. The church as the real Eve is the totality of Christ in all His believers; the church is the reproduction of Christ; other than Christ's element, there should be no other element in the church (Gen. 5:2).

4. Only that which comes out of Christ with His resurrection life can be His complement and counterpart, the Body of Christ (1 Cor. 12:12; Eph. 5:28-30):

   a. We need to put off all the natural life until the living Christ can be expressed from within our spirit; then we will be the church in reality (Col. 3:10-11).

   b. To live out anything other than Christ is not the church; "it is no longer I who live, but it is Christ who lives in me" (Gal. 2:20); "to me, to live is Christ" (Phil. 1:21)—this is the church!

   c. Only that which comes out of Christ can be recognized by Christ; only that which comes out of Christ can return to Christ and match Him.

5. At the end of the Bible is a city, New Jerusalem, the ultimate and eternal woman, the

corporate bride, the wife of the Lamb (Rev. 21:9; 22:17) built with three precious materials (21:18-21), fulfilling for eternity the type shown in Genesis 2; thus, in type all the precious materials mentioned in Genesis 2:11-12 are for the building of the woman.

6. As Eve was taken out of Adam and brought back to Adam to be one flesh with him (v. 24), so the church produced out of Christ will go back to Christ (Eph. 5:27; Rev. 19:7) to be one spirit with Him (1 Cor. 6:17); Christ and the church as one spirit, typified by a husband and wife as one flesh, are the great mystery (Eph. 5:28-32).

7. In the future, Christ as the holy Bridegroom will present us to Himself as His counterpart for His marriage just as God presented Eve to Adam as his counterpart for his marriage (vv. 27, 31-32; Gen. 2:22-24; Rev. 19:7-9):

   a. Ephesians 5:27 reveals the beauty of the bride, saying that Christ will "present the church to Himself glorious, not having spot or wrinkle or any such things, but that she would be holy and without blemish."

   b. The beauty of the bride comes from the very Christ who is wrought into the church and who is then expressed through the church (v. 26; Psa. 45:9-14).

   c. The Lord's recovery is for the preparation of the bride of Christ, who is composed of all the overcomers (Rev. 19:7-9; Gen. 2:22; Matt. 16:18).

E. "The man said, This time this is bone of my bones / And flesh of my flesh; / This one shall be called Woman / Because out of Man this one was taken. Therefore a man shall leave his father and his mother and shall cleave to his wife, and they shall become one flesh" (Gen. 2:23-24):

Day 6   1. In Hebrew *Man* is *Ish,* and *Woman* is *Ish-shah;* the church is a pure product out of Christ; the church is "Christly," "resurrectionly," and heavenly.

2. Only those who are regenerated of Christ and who live by Christ as the church can match Christ and complement Him.

3. When Christ sees this, He surely says, "This time this is bone of My bones and flesh of My flesh" (cf. v. 23; Eph. 5:30).

4. Just as Eve was the increase of Adam, the church as the bride is the increase of Christ as the Bridegroom (John 3:29-30).

5. Adam and Eve becoming one flesh, a complete unit, is a figure of God and man being joined as one; the coming New Jerusalem will be the eternal union of God and man, a universal couple as a complete unit composed of divinity and humanity (cf. Gen. 5:2).

F. Adam and Eve, being one, lived a married life together as husband and wife (2:24-25); this portrays that in the New Jerusalem the processed and consummated redeeming Triune God as the universal Husband will live a married life with the redeemed, regenerated, transformed, and glorified humanity as the wife, forever (Rev. 22:17a):

1. The entire revelation of the Bible shows us the love story of a universal couple.

2. The sovereign Lord, who created the universe and all things, that is, the Triune God— the Father, the Son, and the Spirit—who went through the processes of incarnation, human living, crucifixion, resurrection, and ascension, and who ultimately became the life-giving Spirit, is joined in marriage to the created, redeemed, regenerated, transformed, and glorified tripartite man—composed of spirit, soul, and body—who ultimately constitutes the church, the expression of God.

   3. In the eternity that is without end, by the di-
      vine, eternal, and surpassingly glorious life,
      they will live a life that is the mingling of God
      and man as one spirit, a life that is superex-
      cellent and that overflows with blessings and
      joy.

Morning Nourishment

Jer. ...Thus says Jehovah: I remember concerning you
2:2 the kindness of your youth, the love of your bridal
days, when you followed after Me in the wilderness...
Eph. ...Christ also loved the church and gave Himself
5:25 up for her.
27 That He might present the church to Himself glorious, not having spot or wrinkle or any such things,
but that she would be holy and without blemish.

The mentioning of love [in Exodus 20:6] indicates that God's intention in giving His law to His chosen people was that they become His lovers (Deut. 6:5; Matt. 22:35-38; Mark 12:28-30). In
bringing His people out of Egypt and giving His law to them, God
was courting them, wooing them, and seeking to win their affection. Jeremiah 2:2; 31:32; and Ezekiel 16:8 indicate that the covenant enacted at the mountain of God through the giving of the law
(Exo. 24:7-8; 34:27-28) was an engagement covenant, in which God
betrothed the children of Israel to Himself (cf. 2 Cor. 11:2). The Ten
Commandments, especially the first five, gave the terms of the engagement between God and His people. The highest function of the
law is to bring God's chosen people into oneness with Him, as a wife
is brought into oneness with her husband (cf. Gen. 2:24; Rev. 22:17).
In order for God and His people to be one, there must be a mutual
love between them (John 14:21, 23). The love between God and His
people unfolded in the Bible is primarily like the affectionate love
between a man and a woman (Jer. 2:2; 31:3). As God's people love
God and spend time to fellowship with Him in His word, God infuses them with His divine element, making them one with Him as
His spouse, the same as He is in life, nature, and expression (Gen.
2:18-25 and footnotes). (Exo. 20:6, footnote 2)

Today's Reading

The entire Bible is a divine romance, a record of how God
courts His chosen people and eventually marries them (Gen.
2:21-24; S. S. 1:2-4; Isa. 54:5; 62:5; Jer. 2:2; 3:1, 14; 31:32; Ezek.
16:8; 23:5; Hosea 2:7, 19; Matt. 9:15; John 3:29; 2 Cor. 11:2; Eph.

5:25-32; Rev. 19:7; 21:2, 9-10; 22:17). When we as God's people enter into a love relationship with God, we receive His life, just as Eve received the life of Adam (Gen. 2:21-22). It is this life that enables us to become one with God and makes Him one with us. We keep the law not by exercising our mind and will (cf. Rom. 7:18-25) but by loving the Lord as our Husband and thereby partaking of His life and nature to become one with Him as His enlargement and expression. (Exo. 20:6, footnote 2)

In the past, Christ as the Redeemer gave Himself up for the church (Eph. 5:25) for redemption and the impartation of life (John 19:34); in the present, He as the life-giving Spirit is sanctifying the church through separation, saturation, transformation, growth, and building up; and in the future, He as the Bridegroom will present the church to Himself as His counterpart for His satisfaction. Therefore, Christ's loving the church is to separate and sanctify her, and His separating and sanctifying the church are to present her to Himself. (Eph. 5:27, footnote 1)

Another aspect of the church [is] that of the bride. This aspect reveals that the church comes out of Christ, as Eve came out of Adam (Gen. 2:21-22), that it has the same life and nature as Christ, and that it becomes one with Him as His counterpart, as Eve became one flesh with Adam (Gen. 2:24). (Eph. 5:27, footnote 2)

Humanly speaking, the end of Genesis 2 is easy to understand because it relates the story of a marriage. Adam was created, but he had no wife. Thus, God provided a wife for him....If we read through the whole Bible, we will realize that the marriage found in Genesis 2 is...an allegory....Later in the Old Testament God told His people, "For your Maker is your Husband" (Isa. 54:5). Man's Creator is his Husband, meaning that in the universe the unique man is God Himself. The man created by God actually is not a man, but a woman,...a female,...[a] part of the wife. First, God was my Creator. Second, He became my Redeemer. Now He is my Husband. (*Life-study of Genesis,* pp. 213-214)

Further Reading: Life-study of Genesis, msg. 17

Enlightenment and inspiration: _____

_____

_____

_____

Morning Nourishment

Gen. **And Jehovah God said, It is not good for the man to**
2:18 **be alone; I will make him a helper as his counterpart.**
22 **And Jehovah God built the rib, which He had taken**
   from the man, into a woman and brought her to the
   man.

The third step of God's procedure in fulfilling His purpose was
to work Himself into man to make man His complement. Adam
here [in Genesis 2:18] typifies God in Christ as the real, universal
Husband, who is seeking a wife for Himself (Rom. 5:14; cf. Isa.
54:5; John 3:29; 2 Cor. 11:2; Eph. 5:31-32; Rev. 19:7; 21:9). Adam's
need for a wife typifies and portrays God's need, in His economy,
to have a wife as His complement. (Gen. 2:18, footnote 1)

Today's Reading

Besides Adam in the creation, there was also the woman,
Eve. God very carefully recorded the creation of this woman in
Genesis 2, and when we come to Ephesians 5 we are clearly told
that Eve typifies the church. Therefore, we can see that God's
eternal will is achieved partly through Christ and partly through
the church. In order for us to understand how the church can
achieve God's will on earth, we must learn from Eve.

When we read Genesis 2:18-24 and Ephesians 5:22-32 we find
that a woman is mentioned in both places. In Genesis 2 there is a
woman, and in Ephesians 5 there is also a woman. The first woman is a sign typifying the church; the second woman is the first
woman. The first woman was planned by God before the foundation of the world and appeared before the fall. The second woman
was also planned before the foundation of the world, but was revealed after the fall. Although one appeared before the fall and the
other after, there is no difference in God's sight: the church is the
Eve of Genesis 2. God created Adam to typify Christ; God also created Eve to typify the church. God's purpose is not only accomplished by Christ but is also accomplished by the church. In Genesis 2:18, Jehovah God said, "It is not good for the man to be alone;
I will make him a helper as his counterpart." God's purpose in

creating the church is that she may be the counterpart of Christ. Christ alone is only half; there must be another half, which is the church. God said, "It is not good for the man to be alone." This means that in God's sight Christ alone is not good enough. Genesis 2:18-24 reiterates the events of the sixth day of creation. On the sixth day God created Adam, but afterward it seems that He considered a little and said, "No, it is not good that the man should be alone." Therefore, He created Eve for Adam. By then, everything was completed, and we find that Genesis 1 ends with this record: "And God saw everything that He had made, and indeed, it was very good" (v. 31). From this we realize that having Adam alone, or we may say, having Christ alone, is not enough to satisfy God's heart. With God there must also be Eve, that is, there must also be the church. Then His heart will be satisfied.

The Lord God said, "It is not good for the man to be alone" [v. 18]. In other words, God desired to have both Adam *and Eve*. His purpose is to have a victorious Christ plus a victorious church, a Christ who has overcome the work of the devil plus a church which has overthrown the work of the devil. His purpose is to have a ruling Christ and a ruling church. This is what God planned for His own pleasure, and He has performed it for His own satisfaction. It has been done because God desired to do it. God desired to have Christ, and God also desired to have a church which is exactly like Christ. God not only desired that Christ would have dominion; He also wants the church to have dominion. God allows the devil on earth because He said, "Let them," Christ and the church, "have dominion" [Gen. 1:26]. God purposed that the church, as Christ's counterpart, should take part in dealing with Satan. If the church does not match Christ, God's purpose will not be fulfilled. In warfare Christ needs a counterpart, and even in glory He also needs a counterpart. God requires the church to be the same as Christ in every respect. It is God's desire that Christ should have a counterpart. (*CWWN,* vol. 34, "The Glorious Church," pp. 25-26)

Further Reading: CWWN, vol. 34, "The Glorious Church," ch. 2

Enlightenment and inspiration: _____

_____

_____

_____

Morning Nourishment

Gen.   Now Jehovah God had formed from the ground every
2:19-21 animal of the field and every bird of heaven. And He
brought *them* to the man to see what he would call
them....But for Adam there was not found a helper
as his counterpart. And Jehovah God caused a deep
sleep to fall upon the man, and he slept; and He took
one of his ribs and closed up the flesh in its place.

The wife must be the same as the husband in life, nature, and
expression. Among the cattle, the birds, and the animals Adam
did not find a complement for himself, one that could match him.
(Gen. 2:20, footnote 1)

In order to produce a complement for Himself, God first became
a man (John 1:14), as typified by God's creation of Adam (Rom.
5:14)....Adam's deep sleep for the producing of Eve as his wife typifies Christ's death on the cross for the producing of the church as
His counterpart (Eph. 5:25-27). Through Christ's death the divine
life within Him was released, and through His resurrection His released divine life was imparted into His believers for the constitut-
ing of the church (see footnote 1 on John 19:34). Through such a
process God in Christ has been wrought into man with His life and
nature so that man can be the same as God in life and nature in order to match Him as His counterpart. (Gen. 2:21, footnote 1)

Today's Reading

Adam needed a counterpart. What did God do to meet this
need?...God brought every kind of living creature before Adam, but
Adam could not find his counterpart among them. None of the living creatures made out of earth could be a counterpart for Adam.

Therefore, "Jehovah God caused a deep sleep to fall upon the
man, and he slept; and He took one of his ribs and closed up the
flesh in its place. And Jehovah God built the rib, which He had
taken from the man, into a woman and brought her to the man.
And the man said, This time this is bone of my bones / And flesh
of my flesh; / This one shall be called Woman / Because out of
Man this one was taken" (Gen. 2:21-23). This one was Adam's

counterpart and the figure of the church in Ephesians 5. The Bible says very clearly that all of the things made of earth and not taken out of the body of Adam could not be his counterpart. All the beasts of the field, the cattle, and the birds of the air were made of earth. They were not taken out of Adam; therefore, they could not be the counterpart to Adam. We must remember that Eve was formed out of a rib taken from Adam; therefore, Eve was the constituent of Adam. This means that the church comes out of Christ. Only that which is out of Christ can be the church. Anything that is not of Christ is not the church.

"God said, Let Us make man in Our image, according to Our likeness; and let *them*..." [Gen. 1:26]. In the Hebrew language the word "man" is singular, but immediately following, the plural pronoun "them" is used. The same pattern is used in verse 27 which says, "And God created man in His own image; in the image of God He created him; male and female He created them."...The way God created "man" is the *same way* He created "them." Not only was Adam created, but Eve also was included in him [v. 27]. "God created *man* in His own image." This "man" is singular and typifies Christ. "In the image of God He created...*them*" [v. 27]. "Them" is plural and typifies Christ and the church. God not only wants to have an only begotten Son; He also wants many sons. The many sons must be just like the one Son. From these verses we see that if the church is not in a state which corresponds with Christ, God will not rest and His work will not be completed. Not only is Adam in the image of God; Eve is also in the image of God. Not only does Christ have the life of God; the church also has God's life.

The fact that Eve was made from Adam signifies that the church is made from Christ. Eve was made with Adam's rib. Since Eve came out *from* Adam, she was still Adam. Then what is the church? The church is another form of Christ, just as Eve was another form of Adam. (*CWWN,* vol. 34, "The Glorious Church," pp. 27-28)

Further Reading: CWWN, vol. 34, "The Glorious Church," chs. 2-3

Enlightenment and inspiration: _____

_____

_____

_____

Morning Nourishment

Gen.   ...Jehovah God built the rib, which He had taken from
2:22-24 the man, into a woman and brought her to the man.
         And the man said, This time this is bone of my bones
         and flesh of my flesh; this one shall be called Woman
         because out of Man this one was taken. Therefore a
         man shall leave his father and his mother and shall
         cleave to his wife, and they shall become one flesh.

In Genesis 2 there is the picture of how the bride of Christ comes into being. Before God prepared a bride for Adam, He brought all the animals to Adam, and Adam named each one. But none of these created things matched Adam, and they could not be his counterpart (vv. 19-20). Then God caused a deep sleep to fall upon Adam (v. 21). Adam is a type of Christ (Rom. 5:14), and his sleep is a type of Christ's death. In the Bible sleep means death (1 Cor. 15:18; 1 Thes. 4:13-16; John 11:11-14). (*CWWL, 1969,* vol. 2, "The Crucial Revelation of Life in the Scriptures," p. 401)

Today's Reading

One day the real Adam was put to sleep on the cross where He slept for six hours, from nine o'clock in the morning until three o'clock in the afternoon (Mark 15:25, 33)....[The] sleep of Adam's [in Genesis 2:21] was a type of Christ's death on the cross for producing the church. This is the life-releasing, life-imparting, life-propagating, life-multiplying, and life-reproducing death of Christ, which is signified by a grain of wheat falling into the ground to die and to grow up in order to produce many grains (John 12:24) for the making of the loaf which is the Body, the church (1 Cor. 10:17). By producing the church in this way God in Christ has been wrought into man as life. First, God became a man. Then this man with the divine life and nature was multiplied through death and resurrection into many believers who become the many members to compose the real Eve to match Him and to complement Him. It is through this process that God in Christ has been wrought into man with His life and nature that man in life and nature can be the same as He is in order to match Him as His complement.

At the end of Christ's crucifixion, the Jews, who did not want the bodies of the crucified criminals to remain upon the cross on the Sabbath day, asked Pilate to have their legs broken (John 19:31). When the soldiers came to Jesus to break His legs, they found that He had died already and that there was no need for them to break His bones. This fulfilled the scripture which said, "No bone of His shall be broken" (John 19:36, 32-33; Exo. 12:46; Num. 9:12; Psa. 34:20). Nevertheless, the soldiers pierced His side and blood and water came out (John 19:34). The blood was for redemption (Heb. 9:22; 1 Pet. 1:18-19). What does the water signify? In Exodus 17:6 we find the type of the smitten rock (1 Cor. 10:4). After the rock was smitten, it was cleft, and living water came forth. Jesus on the cross was smitten with the rod of Moses, that is, by the law of God. He was cleft. His side was pierced, and water came forth. This water was the flow of His divine life signifying the life which produces the church.

This life was typified by the rib, a piece of bone taken out of Adam's opened side, of which Eve was produced and built. Hence, the bone typifies the divine life that is signified by the water flowing out of Christ's side. None of His bones was broken. This signifies that His divine life cannot be broken. His physical life was killed, but nothing could break His divine life which flows out to produce the church.

After God finished the work of producing Eve during Adam's sleep, Adam awoke from his sleep. As Adam's sleep typifies the death of Christ, so his waking signifies the resurrection of Christ. After waking, Adam became another person with Eve produced out of him. After His resurrection Christ also became another person with the church brought forth out of Him. As Adam eventually awoke from his sleep to take Eve as his counterpart, so Christ was also resurrected from the dead to take the church as His complement. (*Life-study of Genesis*, pp. 219-220)

Further Reading: CWWL, 1969, vol. 2, "The Crucial Revelation of Life in the Scriptures," ch. 2

Enlightenment and inspiration: _____

_____

_____

_____

Morning Nourishment

John But one of the soldiers pierced His side with a spear,
19:34 and immediately there came out blood and water.
  36 For these things happened that the Scripture might
     be fulfilled: "No bone of His shall be broken."

During Adam's sleep, God took one of his ribs from his side.
Likewise, when Christ was sleeping on the cross, something came
out of His side. John 19:34 tells us that when the soldier pierced
His side, out came blood and water. At Adam's time there was no
sin, so there was no need of redemption. It was not until Genesis 3
that sin came in. Thus, all that came out of Adam's side was the rib
without the blood. However, by the time that Christ was sleeping
on the cross, there was the problem of sin. Thus, His death must
deal with this sin problem. The blood came out of Christ's side for
redemption. Following the blood, the water came out, which is the
flowing life to produce the church. This divine, flowing, uncreated
life is typified by the rib taken out of Adam's side. (*CWWL, 1969,*
vol. 2, "The Crucial Revelation of Life in the Scriptures," p. 401)

Today's Reading

When the Lord Jesus was dying on the cross, two others were
dying with Him. Their legs were broken, but when the soldiers
came to the Lord Jesus, He was already dead, and there was no
need to break His bones. This fulfilled the prophecy that not one
of His bones would be broken (John 19:31-33). Thus, the bone
taken out of Adam's side signifies the Lord's unbroken, unbreakable, resurrection life. His resurrection life is unbreakable.
The rib taken out of Adam signifies the resurrection life, and
God built a woman with the rib of Adam. Now God builds up the
church with the resurrection life of Christ. Just as Eve was a
part of Adam, so the church is a part of Christ. Eve was bone of
Adam's bones and flesh of Adam's flesh. Today we as the church
are a part of Christ (Eph. 5:30-32).

When we received the Lord Jesus, He came into us as the resurrection life, the unbreakable life. It is this life that transforms
us. This life is the tree of life, the river of life, the very life that

supplies us and that flows within us to transform us. Day by day as we enjoy this flowing, divine, uncreated, unbreakable life, we are being transformed. This transformation is mentioned and revealed in Romans 12:2 and 2 Corinthians 3:18. As we are being transformed, we are also being built into the church to be the bride to satisfy Christ as His counterpart. At the end of Genesis 2 is Eve, and at the end of the entire Bible is the New Jerusalem, which is the ultimate Eve, the ultimate consummation of the universal bride built up with precious materials produced by the resurrection life of Christ.

This bride, the New Jerusalem, will fulfill the two aspects of the purpose of God. First, the New Jerusalem will be the full expression of God in God's full image (Rev. 21:11; cf. 4:3). Second, this New Jerusalem will subdue the enemy, conquer the earth, and exercise God's authority over the entire universe, especially over the creeping things (22:5; 21:15; cf. v. 8; 20:10, 14-15).... May we all be brought into the enjoyment and experience of this flowing, transforming, and building life to be prepared as the bride that will bring Christ back. (*CWWL, 1969,* vol. 2, "The Crucial Revelation of Life in the Scriptures," pp. 401-402)

The church is nothing more than a pure product out of Christ. This is typified by Eve in the book of Genesis. Eve was fully, completely, and purely produced out of Adam (Gen. 2:21-24). Within Eve there was nothing else but Adam. Besides the adamic element, there was no other element in Eve. Whatever was in Eve and whatever Eve was, was Adam. Eve was a full reproduction of Adam. Adam and Eve are a type of Christ and the church (Eph. 5:30-32; Gen. 2:22-24). The church must also be one element—the element of Christ. Other than Christ's element there should be no other element in the church.... Anything that is other than Christ is not the church. (*CWWL, 1984,* vol. 2, "Elders' Training, Book 2: The Vision of the Lord's Recovery," p. 115)

Further Reading: CWWL, 1969, vol. 2, "The Crucial Revelation of Life in the Scriptures," ch. 2

Enlightenment and inspiration: _____

_____

_____

_____

Morning Nourishment

John   He who has the bride is the bridegroom....He must
3:29-30 increase, but I *must* decrease.
Rev.   And the Spirit and the bride say, Come! And let him
22:17   who hears say, Come! And let him who is thirsty
         come; let him who wills take the water of life freely.

After Christ terminated the entire old creation through His all-inclusive death, the church was produced in His resurrection (1 Pet. 1:3; Eph. 2:6). The church is an entity absolutely in resurrection; it is not natural, nor is it of the old creation....Ephesians 2:6 tells us that the church has been resurrected with Christ, and now the church is seated in the heavenlies with Christ. Therefore, the church is absolutely and purely of the element of Christ, absolutely in resurrection, and absolutely remaining in the heavenlies with Christ....We may say that today the church is "Christly," "resurrectionly," and heavenly...With the church there is no element other than Christ. Such a vision will govern you to the uttermost and will rule out everything that is not Christly (of Christ), resurrectionly (of resurrection), or heavenly (of the heavens). (*CWWL, 1984,* vol. 2, "Elders' Training, Book 2: The Vision of the Lord's Recovery," pp. 115-116)

Today's Reading

In the same way that Eve was the complement of Adam, the church is the complement of Christ....Only those who are regenerated of Christ and who live by Christ as the church can match Christ and complement Him. When Christ sees this, He surely says, "This time this is bone of my bones and flesh of my flesh" (Gen. 2:23; cf. Eph. 5:30). (*Life-study of Genesis,* p. 218)

Adam and Eve becoming one flesh, one complete unit, is a figure of God and man being joined as one. The coming New Jerusalem will be the eternal union of God and man, a universal couple as a complete unit composed of divinity and humanity. (Gen. 2:24, footnote 1)

Adam and Eve, being one, lived a married life together as husband and wife. This portrays that in the New Jerusalem the processed and consummated redeeming Triune God as the universal Husband will live a married life with the redeemed, regenerated, transformed, and glorified humanity as the wife, forever.

The revelation concerning the garden of Eden, as the beginning of the divine revelation in the Holy Scriptures, and the revelation concerning the New Jerusalem, as the ending of the divine revelation in the Holy Scriptures, reflect each other. Both contain four things: (1) the tree of life as the center of God's eternal economy (Gen. 2:9; Rev. 22:2), (2) the river flowing to reach the four directions of the earth (Gen. 2:10; Rev. 22:1), (3) three kinds of precious materials (Gen. 2:11-12; Rev. 21:11-14...), and (4) a couple (Gen. 2:18-25; Rev. 21:9-10; 22:17). What is revealed in these two parts of the Scriptures is the central line of the divine revelation of the entire Holy Scriptures and should be a controlling principle of the interpreting and understanding of the Holy Scriptures. (Gen. 2:25, footnote 1)

The Spirit and the bride, the church, speaking together as one [in Revelation 22:17]...indicates that the church's experience of the Spirit has improved to the extent that she has become one with the Spirit, who is the ultimate consummation of the Triune God.

The entire revelation of the Bible shows us the love story of a universal couple. That is, the sovereign Lord, who created the universe and all things, the Triune God—the Father, the Son, and the Spirit—who went through the processes of incarnation, human living, crucifixion, resurrection, and ascension, and who ultimately became the life-giving Spirit, is joined in marriage to the created, redeemed, regenerated, transformed, and glorified tripartite man—composed of spirit, soul, and body—who ultimately constitutes the church, the expression of God. In the eternity that is without end, by the divine, eternal, and surpassingly glorious life, they will live a life that is the mingling of God and man as one spirit, a life that is superexcellent and that overflows with blessings and joy. (Rev. 22:17, footnote 1)

Further Reading: CWWL, 1984, vol. 2, "Elders' Training, Book 2: The Vision of the Lord's Recovery," ch. 3

Enlightenment and inspiration: _____

_____

_____

_____

Hymns, #819

1   As the body is the fulness
       To express our life,
    So to Christ the church, His Body,
       Doth express His life.

2   E'en as Eve is part of Adam,
       Taken out of him,
    So the Church is Christ's own increase
       With Himself within.

3   As from out the buried kernel,
       Many grains are formed,
    As the grains together blended
       To a loaf are formed;

4   So the church, of many Christians,
       Christ doth multiply,
    Him expressing as one Body,
       God to glorify.

5   As the branches of the grapevine
       Are its outward spread,
    With it one, abiding, bearing
       Clusters in its stead;

6   So the church's many members
       Christ's enlargement are,
    One with Him in life and living,
       Spreading Him afar.

7   Fulness, increase, duplication,
       His expression full,
    Growth and spread, continuation,
       Surplus plentiful,

8   Is the church to Christ, and thereby
       God in Christ may be
    Glorified through His redeemed ones
       To eternity.

9   Thus the church and Christ together,
       God's great mystery,
    Is the mingling of the Godhead
       With humanity.

Composition for prophecy with main point and sub-points: _____

_____

_____

_____

_____

_____

_____

_____

_____

_____

_____

_____

_____

_____

_____

_____

_____

_____

_____

_____

_____

_____

_____

_____

_____

_____

_____

_____

_____

_____

_____

_____

_____

_____

Reading Schedule for the Recovery Version of the Old Testament with Footnotes

Wk.	Lord's Day	Monday	Tuesday	Wednesday	Thursday	Friday	Saturday
1	Gen. 1:1-5 ☐	1:6-23 ☐	1:24-31 ☐	2:1-9 ☐	2:10-25 ☐	3:1-13 ☐	3:14-24 ☐
2	4:1-26 ☐	5:1-32 ☐	6:1-22 ☐	7:1—8:3 ☐	8:4-22 ☐	9:1-29 ☐	10:1-32 ☐
3	11:1-32 ☐	12:1-20 ☐	13:1-18 ☐	14:1-24 ☐	15:1-21 ☐	16:1-16 ☐	17:1-27 ☐
4	18:1-33 ☐	19:1-38 ☐	20:1-18 ☐	21:1-34 ☐	22:1-24 ☐	23:1—24:27 ☐	24:28-67 ☐
5	25:1-34 ☐	26:1-35 ☐	27:1-46 ☐	28:1-22 ☐	29:1-35 ☐	30:1-43 ☐	31:1-55 ☐
6	32:1-32 ☐	33:1—34:31 ☐	35:1-29 ☐	36:1-43 ☐	37:1-36 ☐	38:1—39:23 ☐	40:1—41:13 ☐
7	41:14-57 ☐	42:1-38 ☐	43:1-34 ☐	44:1-34 ☐	45:1-28 ☐	46:1-34 ☐	47:1-31 ☐
8	48:1-22 ☐	49:1-15 ☐	49:16-33 ☐	50:1-26 ☐	Exo. 1:1-22 ☐	2:1-25 ☐	3:1-22 ☐
9	4:1-31 ☐	5:1-23 ☐	6:1-30 ☐	7:1-25 ☐	8:1-32 ☐	9:1-35 ☐	10:1-29 ☐
10	11:1-10 ☐	12:1-14 ☐	12:15-36 ☐	12:37-51 ☐	13:1-22 ☐	14:1-31 ☐	15:1-27 ☐
11	16:1-36 ☐	17:1-16 ☐	18:1-27 ☐	19:1-25 ☐	20:1-26 ☐	21:1-36 ☐	22:1-31 ☐
12	23:1-33 ☐	24:1-18 ☐	25:1-22 ☐	25:23-40 ☐	26:1-14 ☐	26:15-37 ☐	27:1-21 ☐
13	28:1-21 ☐	28:22-43 ☐	29:1-21 ☐	29:22-46 ☐	30:1-10 ☐	30:11-38 ☐	31:1-17 ☐
14	31:18—32:35 ☐	33:1-23 ☐	34:1-35 ☐	35:1-35 ☐	36:1-38 ☐	37:1-29 ☐	38:1-31 ☐
15	39:1-43 ☐	40:1-38 ☐	Lev. 1:1-17 ☐	2:1-16 ☐	3:1-17 ☐	4:1-35 ☐	5:1-19 ☐
16	6:1-30 ☐	7:1-38 ☐	8:1-36 ☐	9:1-24 ☐	10:1-20 ☐	11:1-47 ☐	12:1-8 ☐
17	13:1-28 ☐	13:29-59 ☐	14:1-18 ☐	14:19-32 ☐	14:33-57 ☐	15:1-33 ☐	16:1-17 ☐
18	16:18-34 ☐	17:1-16 ☐	18:1-30 ☐	19:1-37 ☐	20:1-27 ☐	21:1-24 ☐	22:1-33 ☐
19	23:1-22 ☐	23:23-44 ☐	24:1-23 ☐	25:1-23 ☐	25:24-55 ☐	26:1-24 ☐	26:25-46 ☐
20	27:1-34 ☐	Num. 1:1-54 ☐	2:1-34 ☐	3:1-51 ☐	4:1-49 ☐	5:1-31 ☐	6:1-27 ☐
21	7:1-41 ☐	7:42-88 ☐	7:89—8:26 ☐	9:1-23 ☐	10:1-36 ☐	11:1-35 ☐	12:1—13:33 ☐
22	14:1-45 ☐	15:1-41 ☐	16:1-50 ☐	17:1—18:7 ☐	18:8-32 ☐	19:1-22 ☐	20:1-29 ☐
23	21:1-35 ☐	22:1-41 ☐	23:1-30 ☐	24:1-25 ☐	25:1-18 ☐	26:1-65 ☐	27:1-23 ☐
24	28:1-31 ☐	29:1-40 ☐	30:1—31:24 ☐	31:25-54 ☐	32:1-42 ☐	33:1-56 ☐	34:1-29 ☐
25	35:1-34 ☐	36:1-13 ☐	Deut. 1:1-46 ☐	2:1-37 ☐	3:1-29 ☐	4:1-49 ☐	5:1-33 ☐
26	6:1—7:26 ☐	8:1-20 ☐	9:1-29 ☐	10:1-22 ☐	11:1-32 ☐	12:1-32 ☐	13:1—14:21 ☐

Reading Schedule for the Recovery Version of the Old Testament with Footnotes

Wk.	Lord's Day	Monday	Tuesday	Wednesday	Thursday	Friday	Saturday
27	14:22—15:23 ☐	16:1-22 ☐	17:1—18:8 ☐	18:9—19:21 ☐	20:1—21:17 ☐	21:18—22:30 ☐	23:1-25 ☐
28	24:1-22 ☐	25:1-19 ☐	26:1-19 ☐	27:1-26 ☐	28:1-68 ☐	29:1-29 ☐	30:1—31:29 ☐
29	31:30—32:52 ☐	33:1-29 ☐	34:1-12 ☐	Josh. 1:1-18 ☐	2:1-24 ☐	3:1-17 ☐	4:1-24 ☐
30	5:1-15 ☐	6:1-27 ☐	7:1-26 ☐	8:1-35 ☐	9:1-27 ☐	10:1-43 ☐	11:1—12:24 ☐
31	13:1-33 ☐	14:1—15:63 ☐	16:1—18:28 ☐	19:1-51 ☐	20:1—21:45 ☐	22:1-34 ☐	23:1—24:33 ☐
32	Judg. 1:1-36 ☐	2:1-23 ☐	3:1-31 ☐	4:1-24 ☐	5:1-31 ☐	6:1-40 ☐	7:1-25 ☐
33	8:1-35 ☐	9:1-57 ☐	10:1—11:40 ☐	12:1—13:25 ☐	14:1—15:20 ☐	16:1-31 ☐	17:1—18:31 ☐
34	19:1-30 ☐	20:1-48 ☐	21:1-25 ☐	Ruth 1:1-22 ☐	2:1-23 ☐	3:1-18 ☐	4:1-22 ☐
35	1 Sam. 1:1-28 ☐	2:1-36 ☐	3:1—4:22 ☐	5:1—6:21 ☐	7:1—8:22 ☐	9:1-27 ☐	10:1—11:15 ☐
36	12:1—13:23 ☐	14:1-52 ☐	15:1-35 ☐	16:1-23 ☐	17:1-58 ☐	18:1-30 ☐	19:1-24 ☐
37	20:1-42 ☐	21:1—22:23 ☐	23:1—24:22 ☐	25:1-44 ☐	26:1-25 ☐	27:1—28:25 ☐	29:1—30:31 ☐
38	31:1-13 ☐	2 Sam. 1:1-27 ☐	2:1-32 ☐	3:1-39 ☐	4:1—5:25 ☐	6:1-23 ☐	7:1-29 ☐
39	8:1—9:13 ☐	10:1—11:27 ☐	12:1-31 ☐	13:1-39 ☐	14:1-33 ☐	15:1—16:23 ☐	17:1—18:33 ☐
40	19:1-43 ☐	20:1—21:22 ☐	22:1-51 ☐	23:1-39 ☐	24:1-25 ☐	1 Kings 1:1-19 ☐	1:20-53 ☐
41	2:1-46 ☐	3:1-28 ☐	4:1-34 ☐	5:1—6:38 ☐	7:1-22 ☐	7:23-51 ☐	8:1-36 ☐
42	8:37-66 ☐	9:1-28 ☐	10:1-29 ☐	11:1-43 ☐	12:1-33 ☐	13:1-34 ☐	14:1-31 ☐
43	15:1-34 ☐	16:1—17:24 ☐	18:1-46 ☐	19:1-21 ☐	20:1-43 ☐	21:1—22:53 ☐	2 Kings 1:1-18 ☐
44	2:1—3:27 ☐	4:1-44 ☐	5:1—6:33 ☐	7:1-20 ☐	8:1-29 ☐	9:1-37 ☐	10:1-36 ☐
45	11:1—12:21 ☐	13:1—14:29 ☐	15:1-38 ☐	16:1-20 ☐	17:1-41 ☐	18:1-37 ☐	19:1-37 ☐
46	20:1—21:26 ☐	22:1-20 ☐	23:1-37 ☐	24:1—25:30 ☐	1 Chron. 1:1-54 ☐	2:1—3:24 ☐	4:1—5:26 ☐
47	6:1-81 ☐	7:1-40 ☐	8:1-40 ☐	9:1-44 ☐	10:1—11:47 ☐	12:1-40 ☐	13:1—14:17 ☐
48	15:1—16:43 ☐	17:1-27 ☐	18:1—19:19 ☐	20:1—21:30 ☐	22:1—23:32 ☐	24:1—25:31 ☐	26:1-32 ☐
49	27:1-34 ☐	28:1—29:30 ☐	2 Chron. 1:1-17 ☐	2:1—3:17 ☐	4:1—5:14 ☐	6:1-42 ☐	7:1—8:18 ☐
50	9:1—10:19 ☐	11:1—12:16 ☐	13:1—15:19 ☐	16:1—17:19 ☐	18:1—19:11 ☐	20:1-37 ☐	21:1—22:12 ☐
51	23:1—24:27 ☐	25:1—26:23 ☐	27:1—28:27 ☐	29:1-36 ☐	30:1—31:21 ☐	32:1-33 ☐	33:1—34:33 ☐
52	35:1—36:23 ☐	Ezra 1:1-11 ☐	2:1-70 ☐	3:1—4:24 ☐	5:1—6:22 ☐	7:1-28 ☐	8:1-36 ☐

Reading Schedule for the Recovery Version of the Old Testament with Footnotes

Wk.	Lord's Day	Monday	Tuesday	Wednesday	Thursday	Friday	Saturday
53	9:1—10:44 ☐	Neh. 1:1-11 ☐	2:1—3:32 ☐	4:1—5:19 ☐	6:1-19 ☐	7:1-73 ☐	8:1-18 ☐
54	9:1-20 ☐	9:21-38 ☐	10:1—11:36 ☐	12:1-47 ☐	13:1-31 ☐	Esth. 1:1-22 ☐	2:1—3:15 ☐
55	4:1—5:14 ☐	6:1—7:10 ☐	8:1-17 ☐	9:1—10:3 ☐	Job 1:1-22 ☐	2:1—3:26 ☐	4:1—5:27 ☐
56	6:1—7:21 ☐	8:1—9:35 ☐	10:1—11:20 ☐	12:1—13:28 ☐	14:1—15:35 ☐	16:1—17:16 ☐	18:1—19:29 ☐
57	20:1—21:34 ☐	22:1—23:17 ☐	24:1—25:6 ☐	26:1—27:23 ☐	28:1—29:25 ☐	30:1—31:40 ☐	32:1—33:33 ☐
58	34:1—35:16 ☐	36:1-33 ☐	37:1-24 ☐	38:1-41 ☐	39:1-30 ☐	40:1-24 ☐	41:1-34 ☐
59	42:1-17 ☐	Psa. 1:1-6 ☐	2:1—3:8 ☐	4:1—6:10 ☐	7:1—8:9 ☐	9:1—10:18 ☐	11:1—15:5 ☐
60	16:1—17:15 ☐	18:1-50 ☐	19:1—21:13 ☐	22:1-31 ☐	23:1—24:10 ☐	25:1—27:14 ☐	28:1—30:12 ☐
61	31:1—32:11 ☐	33:1—34:22 ☐	35:1—36:12 ☐	37:1-40 ☐	38:1—39:13 ☐	40:1—41:13 ☐	42:1—43:5 ☐
62	44:1-26 ☐	45:1-17 ☐	46:1—48:14 ☐	49:1—50:23 ☐	51:1—52:9 ☐	53:1—55:23 ☐	56:1—58:11 ☐
63	59:1—61:8 ☐	62:1—64:10 ☐	65:1—67:7 ☐	68:1-35 ☐	69:1—70:5 ☐	71:1—72:20 ☐	73:1—74:23 ☐
64	75:1—77:20 ☐	78:1-72 ☐	79:1—81:16 ☐	82:1—84:12 ☐	85:1—87:7 ☐	88:1—89:52 ☐	90:1—91:16 ☐
65	92:1—94:23 ☐	95:1—97:12 ☐	98:1—101:8 ☐	102:1—103:22 ☐	104:1—105:45 ☐	106:1-48 ☐	107:1-43 ☐
66	108:1—109:31 ☐	110:1—112:10 ☐	113:1—115:18 ☐	116:1—118:29 ☐	119:1-32 ☐	119:33-72 ☐	119:73-120 ☐
67	119:121-176 ☐	120:1—124:8 ☐	125:1—128:6 ☐	129:1—132:18 ☐	133:1—135:21 ☐	136:1—138:8 ☐	139:1—140:13 ☐
68	141:1—144:15 ☐	145:1—147:20 ☐	148:1—150:6 ☐	Prov. 1:1-33 ☐	2:1—3:35 ☐	4:1—5:23 ☐	6:1-35 ☐
69	7:1—8:36 ☐	9:1—10:32 ☐	11:1—12:28 ☐	13:1—14:35 ☐	15:1-33 ☐	16:1-33 ☐	17:1-28 ☐
70	18:1-24 ☐	19:1—20:30 ☐	21:1—22:29 ☐	23:1-35 ☐	24:1—25:28 ☐	26:1—27:27 ☐	28:1—29:27 ☐
71	30:1-33 ☐	31:1-31 ☐	Eccl. 1:1-18 ☐	2:1—3:22 ☐	4:1—5:20 ☐	6:1—7:29 ☐	8:1—9:18 ☐
72	10:1—11:10 ☐	12:1-14 ☐	S.S. 1:1-8 ☐	1:9-17 ☐	2:1-17 ☐	3:1-11 ☐	4:1-8 ☐
73	4:9-16 ☐	5:1-16 ☐	6:1-13 ☐	7:1-13 ☐	8:1-14 ☐	Isa. 1:1-11 ☐	1:12-31 ☐
74	2:1-22 ☐	3:1-26 ☐	4:1-6 ☐	5:1-30 ☐	6:1-13 ☐	7:1-25 ☐	8:1-22 ☐
75	9:1-21 ☐	10:1-34 ☐	11:1—12:6 ☐	13:1-22 ☐	14:1-14 ☐	14:15-32 ☐	15:1—16:14 ☐
76	17:1—18:7 ☐	19:1-25 ☐	20:1—21:17 ☐	22:1-25 ☐	23:1-18 ☐	24:1-23 ☐	25:1-12 ☐
77	26:1-21 ☐	27:1-13 ☐	28:1-29 ☐	29:1-24 ☐	30:1-33 ☐	31:1—32:20 ☐	33:1-24 ☐
78	34:1-17 ☐	35:1-10 ☐	36:1-22 ☐	37:1-38 ☐	38:1—39:8 ☐	40:1-31 ☐	41:1-29 ☐

Reading Schedule for the Recovery Version of the Old Testament with Footnotes

Wk.	Lord's Day	Monday	Tuesday	Wednesday	Thursday	Friday	Saturday
79	42:1-25 ☐	43:1-28 ☐	44:1-28 ☐	45:1-25 ☐	46:1-13 ☐	47:1-15 ☐	48:1-22 ☐
80	49:1-13 ☐	49:14-26 ☐	50:1—51:23 ☐	52:1-15 ☐	53:1-12 ☐	54:1-17 ☐	55:1-13 ☐
81	56:1-12 ☐	57:1-21 ☐	58:1-14 ☐	59:1-21 ☐	60:1-22 ☐	61:1-11 ☐	62:1-12 ☐
82	63:1-19 ☐	64:1-12 ☐	65:1-25 ☐	66:1-24 ☐	Jer. 1:1-19 ☐	2:1-19 ☐	2:20-37 ☐
83	3:1-25 ☐	4:1-31 ☐	5:1-31 ☐	6:1-30 ☐	7:1-34 ☐	8:1-22 ☐	9:1-26 ☐
84	10:1-25 ☐	11:1—12:17 ☐	13:1-27 ☐	14:1-22 ☐	15:1-21 ☐	16:1—17:27 ☐	18:1-23 ☐
85	19:1—20:18 ☐	21:1—22:30 ☐	23:1-40 ☐	24:1—25:38 ☐	26:1—27:22 ☐	28:1—29:32 ☐	30:1-24 ☐
86	31:1-23 ☐	31:24-40 ☐	32:1-44 ☐	33:1-26 ☐	34:1-22 ☐	35:1-19 ☐	36:1-32 ☐
87	37:1-21 ☐	38:1-28 ☐	39:1—40:16 ☐	41:1—42:22 ☐	43:1—44:30 ☐	45:1—46:28 ☐	47:1—48:16 ☐
88	48:17-47 ☐	49:1-22 ☐	49:23-39 ☐	50:1-27 ☐	50:28-46 ☐	51:1-27 ☐	51:28-64 ☐
89	52:1-34 ☐	Lam. 1:1-22 ☐	2:1-22 ☐	3:1-39 ☐	3:40-66 ☐	4:1-22 ☐	5:1-22 ☐
90	Ezek. 1:1-14 ☐	1:15-28 ☐	2:1—3:27 ☐	4:1—5:17 ☐	6:1—7:27 ☐	8:1—9:11 ☐	10:1—11:25 ☐
91	12:1—13:23 ☐	14:1—15:8 ☐	16:1-63 ☐	17:1—18:32 ☐	19:1-14 ☐	20:1-49 ☐	21:1-32 ☐
92	22:1-31 ☐	23:1-49 ☐	24:1-27 ☐	25:1—26:21 ☐	27:1-36 ☐	28:1-26 ☐	29:1—30:26 ☐
93	31:1—32:32 ☐	33:1-33 ☐	34:1-31 ☐	35:1—36:21 ☐	36:22-38 ☐	37:1-28 ☐	38:1—39:29 ☐
94	40:1-27 ☐	40:28-49 ☐	41:1-26 ☐	42:1—43:27 ☐	44:1-31 ☐	45:1-25 ☐	46:1-24 ☐
95	47:1-23 ☐	48:1-35 ☐	Dan. 1:1-21 ☐	2:1-30 ☐	2:31-49 ☐	3:1-30 ☐	4:1-37 ☐
96	5:1-31 ☐	6:1-28 ☐	7:1-12 ☐	7:13-28 ☐	8:1-27 ☐	9:1-27 ☐	10:1-21 ☐
97	11:1-22 ☐	11:23-45 ☐	12:1-13 ☐	Hosea 1:1-11 ☐	2:1-23 ☐	3:1—4:19 ☐	5:1-15 ☐
98	6:1-11 ☐	7:1-16 ☐	8:1-14 ☐	9:1-17 ☐	10:1-15 ☐	11:1-12 ☐	12:1-14 ☐
99	13:1—14:9 ☐	Joel 1:1-20 ☐	2:1-16 ☐	2:17-32 ☐	3:1-21 ☐	Amos 1:1-15 ☐	2:1-16 ☐
100	3:1-15 ☐	4:1—5:27 ☐	6:1—7:17 ☐	8:1—9:15 ☐	Obad. 1-21 ☐	Jonah 1:1-17 ☐	2:1—4:11 ☐
101	Micah 1:1-16 ☐	2:1—3:12 ☐	4:1—5:15 ☐	6:1—7:20 ☐	Nahum 1:1-15 ☐	2:1—3:19 ☐	Hab. 1:1-17 ☐
102	2:1-20 ☐	3:1-19 ☐	Zeph. 1:1-18 ☐	2:1-15 ☐	3:1-20 ☐	Hag. 1:1-15 ☐	2:1-23 ☐
103	Zech. 1:1-21 ☐	2:1-13 ☐	3:1-10 ☐	4:1-14 ☐	5:1—6:15 ☐	7:1—8:23 ☐	9:1-17 ☐
104	10:1—11:17 ☐	12:1—13:9 ☐	14:1-21 ☐	Mal. 1:1-14 ☐	2:1-17 ☐	3:1-18 ☐	4:1-6 ☐

Reading Schedule for the Recovery Version of the New Testament with Footnotes

Wk.	Lord's Day	Monday	Tuesday	Wednesday	Thursday	Friday	Saturday
1	Matt. 1:1-2 ☐	1:3-7 ☐	1:8-17 ☐	1:18-25 ☐	2:1-23 ☐	3:1-6 ☐	3:7-17 ☐
2	4:1-11 ☐	4:12-25 ☐	5:1-4 ☐	5:5-12 ☐	5:13-20 ☐	5:21-26 ☐	5:27-48 ☐
3	6:1-8 ☐	6:9-18 ☐	6:19-34 ☐	7:1-12 ☐	7:13-29 ☐	8:1-13 ☐	8:14-22 ☐
4	8:23-34 ☐	9:1-13 ☐	9:14-17 ☐	9:18-34 ☐	9:35—10:5 ☐	10:6-25 ☐	10:26-42 ☐
5	11:1-15 ☐	11:16-30 ☐	12:1-14 ☐	12:15-32 ☐	12:33-42 ☐	12:43—13:2 ☐	13:3-12 ☐
6	13:13-30 ☐	13:31-43 ☐	13:44-58 ☐	14:1-13 ☐	14:14-21 ☐	14:22-36 ☐	15:1-20 ☐
7	15:21-31 ☐	15:32-39 ☐	16:1-12 ☐	16:13-20 ☐	16:21-28 ☐	17:1-13 ☐	17:14-27 ☐
8	18:1-14 ☐	18:15-22 ☐	18:23-35 ☐	19:1-15 ☐	19:16-30 ☐	20:1-16 ☐	20:17-34 ☐
9	21:1-11 ☐	21:12-22 ☐	21:23-32 ☐	21:33-46 ☐	22:1-22 ☐	22:23-33 ☐	22:34-46 ☐
10	23:1-12 ☐	23:13-39 ☐	24:1-14 ☐	24:15-31 ☐	24:32-51 ☐	25:1-13 ☐	25:14-30 ☐
11	25:31-46 ☐	26:1-16 ☐	26:17-35 ☐	26:36-46 ☐	26:47-64 ☐	26:65-75 ☐	27:1-26 ☐
12	27:27-44 ☐	27:45-56 ☐	27:57—28:15 ☐	28:16-20 ☐	Mark 1:1 ☐	1:2-6 ☐	1:7-13 ☐
13	1:14-28 ☐	1:29-45 ☐	2:1-12 ☐	2:13-28 ☐	3:1-19 ☐	3:20-35 ☐	4:1-25 ☐
14	4:26-41 ☐	5:1-20 ☐	5:21-43 ☐	6:1-29 ☐	6:30-56 ☐	7:1-23 ☐	7:24-37 ☐
15	8:1-26 ☐	8:27—9:1 ☐	9:2-29 ☐	9:30-50 ☐	10:1-16 ☐	10:17-34 ☐	10:35-52 ☐
16	11:1-16 ☐	11:17-33 ☐	12:1-27 ☐	12:28-44 ☐	13:1-13 ☐	13:14-37 ☐	14:1-26 ☐
17	14:27-52 ☐	14:53-72 ☐	15:1-15 ☐	15:16-47 ☐	16:1-8 ☐	16:9-20 ☐	Luke 1:1-4 ☐
18	1:5-25 ☐	1:26-46 ☐	1:47-56 ☐	1:57-80 ☐	2:1-8 ☐	2:9-20 ☐	2:21-39 ☐
19	2:40-52 ☐	3:1-20 ☐	3:21-38 ☐	4:1-13 ☐	4:14-30 ☐	4:31-44 ☐	5:1-26 ☐
20	5:27—6:16 ☐	6:17-38 ☐	6:39-49 ☐	7:1-17 ☐	7:18-23 ☐	7:24-35 ☐	7:36-50 ☐
21	8:1-15 ☐	8:16-25 ☐	8:26-39 ☐	8:40-56 ☐	9:1-17 ☐	9:18-26 ☐	9:27-36 ☐
22	9:37-50 ☐	9:51-62 ☐	10:1-11 ☐	10:12-24 ☐	10:25-37 ☐	10:38-42 ☐	11:1-13 ☐
23	11:14-26 ☐	11:27-36 ☐	11:37-54 ☐	12:1-12 ☐	12:13-21 ☐	12:22-34 ☐	12:35-48 ☐
24	12:49-59 ☐	13:1-9 ☐	13:10-17 ☐	13:18-30 ☐	13:31—14:6 ☐	14:7-14 ☐	14:15-24 ☐
25	14:25-35 ☐	15:1-10 ☐	15:11-21 ☐	15:22-32 ☐	16:1-13 ☐	16:14-22 ☐	16:23-31 ☐
26	17:1-19 ☐	17:20-37 ☐	18:1-14 ☐	18:15-30 ☐	18:31-43 ☐	19:1-10 ☐	19:11-27 ☐

Reading Schedule for the Recovery Version of the New Testament with Footnotes

Wk.	Lord's Day	Monday	Tuesday	Wednesday	Thursday	Friday	Saturday
27	Luke 19:28-48 ☐	20:1-19 ☐	20:20-38 ☐	20:39—21:4 ☐	21:5-27 ☐	21:28-38 ☐	22:1-20 ☐
28	22:21-38 ☐	22:39-54 ☐	22:55-71 ☐	23:1-43 ☐	23:44-56 ☐	24:1-12 ☐	24:13-35 ☐
29	24:36-53 ☐	John 1:1-13 ☐	1:14-18 ☐	1:19-34 ☐	1:35-51 ☐	2:1-11 ☐	2:12-22 ☐
30	2:23—3:13 ☐	3:14-21 ☐	3:22-36 ☐	4:1-14 ☐	4:15-26 ☐	4:27-42 ☐	4:43-54 ☐
31	5:1-16 ☐	5:17-30 ☐	5:31-47 ☐	6:1-15 ☐	6:16-31 ☐	6:32-51 ☐	6:52-71 ☐
32	7:1-9 ☐	7:10-24 ☐	7:25-36 ☐	7:37-52 ☐	7:53—8:11 ☐	8:12-27 ☐	8:28-44 ☐
33	8:45-59 ☐	9:1-13 ☐	9:14-34 ☐	9:35—10:9 ☐	10:10-30 ☐	10:31—11:4 ☐	11:5-22 ☐
34	11:23-40 ☐	11:41-57 ☐	12:1-11 ☐	12:12-24 ☐	12:25-36 ☐	12:37-50 ☐	13:1-11 ☐
35	13:12-30 ☐	13:31-38 ☐	14:1-6 ☐	14:7-20 ☐	14:21-31 ☐	15:1-11 ☐	15:12-27 ☐
36	16:1-15 ☐	16:16-33 ☐	17:1-5 ☐	17:6-13 ☐	17:14-24 ☐	17:25—18:11 ☐	18:12-27 ☐
37	18:28-40 ☐	19:1-16 ☐	19:17-30 ☐	19:31-42 ☐	20:1-13 ☐	20:14-18 ☐	20:19-22 ☐
38	20:23-31 ☐	21:1-14 ☐	21:15-22 ☐	21:23-25 ☐	Acts 1:1-8 ☐	1:9-14 ☐	1:15-26 ☐
39	2:1-13 ☐	2:14-21 ☐	2:22-36 ☐	2:37-41 ☐	2:42-47 ☐	3:1-18 ☐	3:19—4:22 ☐
40	4:23-37 ☐	5:1-16 ☐	5:17-32 ☐	5:33-42 ☐	6:1—7:1 ☐	7:2-29 ☐	7:30-60 ☐
41	8:1-13 ☐	8:14-25 ☐	8:26-40 ☐	9:1-19 ☐	9:20-43 ☐	10:1-16 ☐	10:17-33 ☐
42	10:34-48 ☐	11:1-18 ☐	11:19-30 ☐	12:1-25 ☐	13:1-12 ☐	13:13-43 ☐	13:44—14:5 ☐
43	14:6-28 ☐	15:1-12 ☐	15:13-34 ☐	15:35—16:5 ☐	16:6-18 ☐	16:19-40 ☐	17:1-18 ☐
44	17:19-34 ☐	18:1-17 ☐	18:18-28 ☐	19:1-20 ☐	19:21-41 ☐	20:1-12 ☐	20:13-38 ☐
45	21:1-14 ☐	21:15-26 ☐	21:27-40 ☐	22:1-21 ☐	22:22-29 ☐	22:30—23:11 ☐	23:12-15 ☐
46	23:16-30 ☐	23:31—24:21 ☐	24:22—25:5 ☐	25:6-27 ☐	26:1-13 ☐	26:14-32 ☐	27:1-26 ☐
47	27:27—28:10 ☐	28:11-22 ☐	28:23-31 ☐	Rom. 1:1-2 ☐	1:3-7 ☐	1:8-17 ☐	1:18-25 ☐
48	1:26—2:10 ☐	2:11-29 ☐	3:1-20 ☐	3:21-31 ☐	4:1-12 ☐	4:13-25 ☐	5:1-11 ☐
49	5:12-17 ☐	5:18—6:5 ☐	6:6-11 ☐	6:12-23 ☐	7:1-12 ☐	7:13-25 ☐	8:1-2 ☐
50	8:3-6 ☐	8:7-13 ☐	8:14-25 ☐	8:26-39 ☐	9:1-18 ☐	9:19—10:3 ☐	10:4-15 ☐
51	10:16—11:10 ☐	11:11-22 ☐	11:23-36 ☐	12:1-3 ☐	12:4-21 ☐	13:1-14 ☐	14:1-12 ☐
52	14:13-23 ☐	15:1-13 ☐	15:14-33 ☐	16:1-5 ☐	16:6-24 ☐	16:25-27 ☐	1 Cor. 1:1-4 ☐

Reading Schedule for the Recovery Version of the New Testament with Footnotes

Wk.	Lord's Day	Monday	Tuesday	Wednesday	Thursday	Friday	Saturday
53	1 Cor. 1:5-9 ☐	1:10-17 ☐	1:18-31 ☐	2:1-5 ☐	2:6-10 ☐	2:11-16 ☐	3:1-9 ☐
54	3:10-13 ☐	3:14-23 ☐	4:1-9 ☐	4:10-21 ☐	5:1-13 ☐	6:1-11 ☐	6:12-20 ☐
55	7:1-16 ☐	7:17-24 ☐	7:25-40 ☐	8:1-13 ☐	9:1-15 ☐	9:16-27 ☐	10:1-4 ☐
56	10:5-13 ☐	10:14-33 ☐	11:1-6 ☐	11:7-16 ☐	11:17-26 ☐	11:27-34 ☐	12:1-11 ☐
57	12:12-22 ☐	12:23-31 ☐	13:1-13 ☐	14:1-12 ☐	14:13-25 ☐	14:26-33 ☐	14:34-40 ☐
58	15:1-19 ☐	15:20-28 ☐	15:29-34 ☐	15:35-49 ☐	15:50-58 ☐	16:1-9 ☐	16:10-24 ☐
59	2 Cor. 1:1-4 ☐	1:5-14 ☐	1:15-22 ☐	1:23—2:11 ☐	2:12-17 ☐	3:1-6 ☐	3:7-11 ☐
60	3:12-18 ☐	4:1-6 ☐	4:7-12 ☐	4:13-18 ☐	5:1-8 ☐	5:9-15 ☐	5:16-21 ☐
61	6:1-13 ☐	6:14—7:4 ☐	7:5-16 ☐	8:1-15 ☐	8:16-24 ☐	9:1-15 ☐	10:1-6 ☐
62	10:7-18 ☐	11:1-15 ☐	11:16-33 ☐	12:1-10 ☐	12:11-21 ☐	13:1-10 ☐	13:11-14 ☐
63	Gal. 1:1-5 ☐	1:6-14 ☐	1:15-24 ☐	2:1-13 ☐	2:14-21 ☐	3:1-4 ☐	3:5-14 ☐
64	3:15-22 ☐	3:23-29 ☐	4:1-7 ☐	4:8-20 ☐	4:21-31 ☐	5:1-12 ☐	5:13-21 ☐
65	5:22-26 ☐	6:1-10 ☐	6:11-15 ☐	6:16-18 ☐	Eph. 1:1-3 ☐	1:4-6 ☐	1:7-10 ☐
66	1:11-14 ☐	1:15-18 ☐	1:19-23 ☐	2:1-5 ☐	2:6-10 ☐	2:11-14 ☐	2:15-18 ☐
67	2:19-22 ☐	3:1-7 ☐	3:8-13 ☐	3:14-18 ☐	3:19-21 ☐	4:1-4 ☐	4:5-10 ☐
68	4:11-16 ☐	4:17-24 ☐	4:25-32 ☐	5:1-10 ☐	5:11-21 ☐	5:22-26 ☐	5:27-33 ☐
69	6:1-9 ☐	6:10-14 ☐	6:15-18 ☐	6:19-24 ☐	Phil. 1:1-7 ☐	1:8-18 ☐	1:19-26 ☐
70	1:27—2:4 ☐	2:5-11 ☐	2:12-16 ☐	2:17-30 ☐	3:1-6 ☐	3:7-11 ☐	3:12-16 ☐
71	3:17-21 ☐	4:1-9 ☐	4:10-23 ☐	Col. 1:1-8 ☐	1:9-13 ☐	1:14-23 ☐	1:24-29 ☐
72	2:1-7 ☐	2:8-15 ☐	2:16-23 ☐	3:1-4 ☐	3:5-15 ☐	3:16-25 ☐	4:1-18 ☐
73	1 Thes. 1:1-3 ☐	1:4-10 ☐	2:1-12 ☐	2:13—3:5 ☐	3:6-13 ☐	4:1-10 ☐	4:11—5:11 ☐
74	5:12-28 ☐	2 Thes. 1:1-12 ☐	2:1-17 ☐	3:1-18 ☐	1 Tim. 1:1-2 ☐	1:3-4 ☐	1:5-14 ☐
75	1:15-20 ☐	2:1-7 ☐	2:8-15 ☐	3:1-13 ☐	3:14—4:5 ☐	4:6-16 ☐	5:1-25 ☐
76	6:1-10 ☐	6:11-21 ☐	2 Tim. 1:1-10 ☐	1:11-18 ☐	2:1-15 ☐	2:16-26 ☐	3:1-13 ☐
77	3:14—4:8 ☐	4:9-22 ☐	Titus 1:1-4 ☐	1:5-16 ☐	2:1-15 ☐	3:1-8 ☐	3:9-15 ☐
78	Philem. 1:1-11 ☐	1:12-25 ☐	Heb. 1:1-2 ☐	1:3-5 ☐	1:6-14 ☐	2:1-9 ☐	2:10-18 ☐

Reading Schedule for the Recovery Version of the New Testament with Footnotes

Wk.	Lord's Day	Monday	Tuesday	Wednesday	Thursday	Friday	Saturday
79	Heb. 3:1-6 ☐	3:7-19 ☐	4:1-9 ☐	4:10-13 ☐	4:14-16 ☐	5:1-10 ☐	5:11—6:3 ☐
80	6:4-8 ☐	6:9-20 ☐	7:1-10 ☐	7:11-28 ☐	8:1-6 ☐	8:7-13 ☐	9:1-4 ☐
81	9:5-14 ☐	9:15-28 ☐	10:1-18 ☐	10:19-28 ☐	10:29-39 ☐	11:1-6 ☐	11:7-19 ☐
82	11:20-31 ☐	11:32-40 ☐	12:1-2 ☐	12:3-13 ☐	12:14-17 ☐	12:18-26 ☐	12:27-29 ☐
83	13:1-7 ☐	13:8-12 ☐	13:13-15 ☐	13:16-25 ☐	James 1:1-8 ☐	1:9-18 ☐	1:19-27 ☐
84	2:1-13 ☐	2:14-26 ☐	3:1-18 ☐	4:1-10 ☐	4:11-17 ☐	5:1-12 ☐	5:13-20 ☐
85	1 Pet. 1:1-2 ☐	1:3-4 ☐	1:5 ☐	1:6-9 ☐	1:10-12 ☐	1:13-17 ☐	1:18-25 ☐
86	2:1-3 ☐	2:4-8 ☐	2:9-17 ☐	2:18-25 ☐	3:1-13 ☐	3:14-22 ☐	4:1-6 ☐
87	4:7-16 ☐	4:17-19 ☐	5:1-4 ☐	5:5-9 ☐	5:10-14 ☐	2 Pet. 1:1-2 ☐	1:3-4 ☐
88	1:5-8 ☐	1:9-11 ☐	1:12-18 ☐	1:19-21 ☐	2:1-3 ☐	2:4-11 ☐	2:12-22 ☐
89	3:1-6 ☐	3:7-9 ☐	3:10-12 ☐	3:13-15 ☐	3:16 ☐	3:17-18 ☐	1 John 1:1-2 ☐
90	1:3-4 ☐	1:5 ☐	1:6 ☐	1:7 ☐	1:8-10 ☐	2:1-2 ☐	2:3-11 ☐
91	2:12-14 ☐	2:15-19 ☐	2:20-23 ☐	2:24-27 ☐	2:28-29 ☐	3:1-5 ☐	3:6-10 ☐
92	3:11-18 ☐	3:19-24 ☐	4:1-6 ☐	4:7-11 ☐	4:12-15 ☐	4:16—5:3 ☐	5:4-13 ☐
93	5:14-17 ☐	5:18-21 ☐	2 John 1:1-3 ☐	1:4-9 ☐	1:10-13 ☐	3 John 1:1-6 ☐	1:7-14 ☐
94	Jude 1:1-4 ☐	1:5-10 ☐	1:11-19 ☐	1:20-25 ☐	Rev. 1:1-3 ☐	1:4-6 ☐	1:7-11 ☐
95	1:12-13 ☐	1:14-16 ☐	1:17-20 ☐	2:1-6 ☐	2:7 ☐	2:8-9 ☐	2:10-11 ☐
96	2:12-14 ☐	2:15-17 ☐	2:18-23 ☐	2:24-29 ☐	3:1-3 ☐	3:4-6 ☐	3:7-9 ☐
97	3:10-13 ☐	3:14-18 ☐	3:19-22 ☐	4:1-5 ☐	4:6-7 ☐	4:8-11 ☐	5:1-6 ☐
98	5:7-14 ☐	6:1-8 ☐	6:9-17 ☐	7:1-8 ☐	7:9-17 ☐	8:1-6 ☐	8:7-12 ☐
99	8:13—9:11 ☐	9:12-21 ☐	10:1-4 ☐	10:5-11 ☐	11:1-4 ☐	11:5-14 ☐	11:15-19 ☐
100	12:1-4 ☐	12:5-9 ☐	12:10-18 ☐	13:1-10 ☐	13:11-18 ☐	14:1-5 ☐	14:6-12 ☐
101	14:13-20 ☐	15:1-8 ☐	16:1-12 ☐	16:13-21 ☐	17:1-6 ☐	17:7-18 ☐	18:1-8 ☐
102	18:9—19:4 ☐	19:5-10 ☐	19:11-16 ☐	19:17-21 ☐	20:1-6 ☐	20:7-10 ☐	20:11-15 ☐
103	21:1 ☐	21:2 ☐	21:3-8 ☐	21:9-13 ☐	21:14-18 ☐	21:19-21 ☐	21:22-27 ☐
104	22:1 ☐	22:2 ☐	22:3-11 ☐	22:12-15 ☐	22:16-17 ☐	22:18-21 ☐	

Week 1 — Day 6   Today's verses

Eph. To me, less than the least of all saints, was
3:8-9 this grace given to announce to the Gentiles the unsearchable riches of Christ as the gospel and to enlighten all *that they may see* what the economy of the mystery is, which throughout the ages has been hidden in God, who created all things.

Date

Week 1 — Day 5   Today's verses

Eph. That by revelation the mystery was made
3:3-5 known to me, as I have written previously in brief, by which, in reading *it*, you can perceive my understanding in the mystery of Christ, which in other generations was not made known to the sons of men, as it has now been revealed to His holy apostles and prophets in spirit.

Date

Week 1 — Day 4   Today's verses

Eph. And to enlighten all *that they may see*
3:9 what the economy of the mystery is, which throughout the ages has been hidden in God, who created all things.

5:32 This mystery is great, but I speak with regard to Christ and the church.

Date

Week 1 — Day 3   Today's verses

Rev. You are worthy, our Lord and God, to re-
4:11 ceive the glory and the honor and the power, for You have created all things, and because of Your will they were, and were created.

2 Cor. The grace of the Lord Jesus Christ and the
13:14 love of God and the fellowship of the Holy Spirit be with you all.

Date

Week 1 — Day 2   Today's verses

Eph. In order that now to the rulers and the au-
3:10-11 thorities in the heavenlies the multifarious wisdom of God might be made known through the church, according to the eternal purpose which He made in Christ Jesus our Lord.

Date

Week 1 — Day 1   Today's verses

Eph. Even as He chose us in Him before the
1:4 foundation of the world to be holy and without blemish before Him in love.

11 In whom also we were designated as an inheritance, having been predestinated according to the purpose of the One who works all things according to the counsel of His will.

Date

Week 2 — Day 4 Today's verses

Rev. I know your works; behold, I have put be-
3:8 fore you an opened door which no one can shut, because you have a little power and have kept My word and have not denied My name.

1 Tim. ...Our Savior God, who desires all men to
2:3-4 be saved and to come to the full knowledge of the truth.

_____
Date

Week 2 — Day 5 Today's verses

1 Cor. The cup of blessing which we bless, is it
10:16-17 not the fellowship of the blood of Christ? The bread which we break, is it not the fellowship of the body of Christ? Seeing that there is one bread, we who are many are one Body; for we all partake of the one bread.

_____
Date

Week 2 — Day 6 Today's verses

Matt. Another parable He spoke to them: The
13:33 kingdom of the heavens is like leaven, which a woman took and hid in three measures of meal until the whole was leavened.

Rev. ...I heard another voice out of heaven,
18:4 saying, Come out of her, My people, that you do not participate in her sins and that you do not receive her plagues.

_____
Date

Week 2 — Day 1 Today's verses

Eph. In order that now to the rulers and the au-
3:10-11 thorities in the heavenlies the multifarious wisdom of God might be made known through the church, according to the eternal purpose which He made in Christ Jesus our Lord.

_____
Date

Week 2 — Day 2 Today's verses

Matt. But you, do not be called Rabbi; for One
23:8 is your Teacher, and you are all brothers.

Rom. And do not be fashioned according to this
12:2 age, but be transformed by the renewing of the mind that you may prove what the will of God is, that which is good and well pleasing and perfect.

_____
Date

Week 2 — Day 3 Today's verses

Acts Now there were in Antioch, in the local
13:1-2 church, prophets and teachers....And as they were ministering to the Lord and fasting, the Holy Spirit said, Set apart for Me now Barnabas and Saul for the work to which I have called them.

_____
Date

Week 3 — Day 4 — Today's verses

Rev. ...He cried with a strong voice, saying,
18:2 Fallen, fallen is Babylon the Great! And she has become a dwelling place of demons and a hold of every unclean spirit and a hold of every unclean and hateful bird.

4 ...I heard another voice out of heaven, saying, Come out of her, My people, that you do not participate in her sins and that you do not receive her plagues.

Week 3 — Day 5 — Today's verses

Lev. If his offering is a burnt offering from the
1:3-4 herd, he shall present it, a male without blemish; he shall present it at the entrance of the Tent of Meeting, that he may be accepted before Jehovah. And he shall lay his hand on the head of the burnt offering, and it shall be accepted for him, to make expiation for him.

Week 3 — Day 6 — Today's verses

Lev. ...This is the law of the burnt offering: The
6:9-10 burnt offering shall be on the hearth on the altar all night until the morning....And the priest shall put on his linen garment;...and he shall take up the ashes to which the fire has consumed the burnt offering on the altar, and he shall put them beside the altar.

12-13 ...The fire on the altar shall be kept burning on...the altar continually; it shall not go out.

Week 3 — Day 1 — Today's verses

Gen. And they said to one another, Come, let
11:3-4 us make bricks and burn *them* thoroughly. And they had brick for stone, and they had tar for mortar. And they said, Come, let us build ourselves a city and a tower whose top is in the heavens; and let us make a name for ourselves, lest we be scattered over the surface of the whole earth.

Week 3 — Day 2 — Today's verses

Rev. As much as she has glorified herself and
18:7 lived luxuriously, as much torment and sorrow give to her; for she says in her heart, I sit a queen, and I am not a widow, and I shall by no means see sorrow.

17:5 And on her forehead there was a name written, MYSTERY, BABYLON THE GREAT, THE MOTHER OF THE HARLOTS AND THE ABOMINATIONS OF THE EARTH.

Week 3 — Day 3 — Today's verses

Rev. I know your works; behold, I have put be-
3:8 fore you an opened door which no one can shut, because you have a little power and have kept My word and have not denied My name.

17:4 And the woman was clothed in purple and scarlet, and gilded with gold and precious stone and pearls, having in her hand a golden cup full of abominations and the unclean things of her fornication.

Week 4 — Day 4   Today's verses

Neh. And all the people gathered as one man....
8:1-3 And Ezra the priest brought the law before the assembly....And he read in it....And the ears of all the people were *attentive* to the book of the law.

7-8 ...And the Levites helped the people understand the law;...and they read in the book, in the law of God, interpreting and giving the sense, so that they understood the reading.

_____
Date

Week 4 — Day 5   Today's verses

Neh. Thus I cleansed them from everything foreign. And I appointed duties for the priests
13:30 and the Levites, each in his work.

Psa. There is a river whose streams gladden the city of God, the holy place of the tabernacles
46:4-5 of the Most High. God is in the midst of her; she will not be moved...

Rev. And have made them a kingdom and
5:10 priests to our God; and they will reign on the earth.

_____
Date

Week 4 — Day 6   Today's verses

Neh. ...The God of heaven Himself will make
2:20 us prosper; therefore we His servants will rise up and build...

Acts Having therefore obtained the help which
26:22 is from God, I have stood unto this day, testifying both to small and great, saying nothing apart from the things which both the prophets and Moses have said would take place.

_____
Date

Week 4 — Day 1   Today's verses

Deut. ...To the place which Jehovah your God will
12:5 choose,...to His habitation,...there shall you go.

11-12 Then to the place where Jehovah your God will choose to cause His name to dwell, there you shall bring...your burnt offerings and your sacrifices, your tithes and the heave offering of your hand and all your choice vows which you vow to Jehovah. And you shall rejoice before Jehovah your God...

_____
Date

Week 4 — Day 2   Today's verses

Ezra Thus says Cyrus the king of Persia, All the
1:2-3 kingdoms of the earth has Jehovah the God of heaven given to me; and He has charged me to build Him a house in Jerusalem, which is in Judah. Whoever there is among you of all His people, may his God be with him; and let him go up to Jerusalem, which is in Judah, and let him build the house of Jehovah the God of Israel—He is God—who is in Jerusalem.

_____
Date

Week 4 — Day 3   Today's verses

Ezra This Ezra went up from Babylon, and he
7:6-7 was a scribe skilled in the law of Moses, which Jehovah the God of Israel had given; and the king granted him all his request according to the hand of Jehovah his God upon him. Some of the children of Israel and some of the priests, and the Levites and the singers and the gatekeepers and the temple servants also went up to Jerusalem...

_____
Date

| Week 5 — Day 4 | Today's verses |

Eph. Unto the economy of the fullness of the
1:10 times, to head up all things in Christ, the
things in the heavens and the things on
the earth, in Him.

4:15 But holding to truth in love, we may grow
up into Him in all things, who is the
Head, Christ.

_____
Date

| Week 5 — Day 5 | Today's verses |

1 Cor. God is faithful, through whom you were
1:9 called into the fellowship of His Son, Jesus
Christ our Lord.

Eph. To Him be the glory in the church and in
3:21 Christ Jesus unto all the generations forever and ever. Amen.

_____
Date

| Week 5 — Day 6 | Today's verses |

John In this is My Father glorified, that you bear
15:8 much fruit and so you will become My
disciples.

Eph. And that you be renewed in the spirit of
4:23 your mind.

_____
Date

| Week 5 — Day 1 | Today's verses |

Matt. And I also say to you that you are Peter,
16:18 and upon this rock I will build My church,
and the gates of Hades shall not prevail
against it.

Rev. Saying, What you see write in a scroll and
1:11 send it to the seven churches: to Ephesus
and to Smyrna and to Pergamos and to
Thyatira and to Sardis and to Philadelphia
and to Laodicea.

_____
Date

| Week 5 — Day 2 | Today's verses |

Gal. I am crucified with Christ; and it is no longer I
2:20 who live, but it is Christ who lives in me; and
the life which I now live in the flesh I live in
faith, the faith of the Son of God, who loved
me and gave Himself up for me.

Col. When Christ our life is manifested, then
3:4 you also will be manifested with Him in
glory.

_____
Date

| Week 5 — Day 3 | Today's verses |

Rom. And do not be fashioned according to this
12:2 age, but be transformed by the renewing
of the mind that you may prove what the
will of God is, that which is good and well
pleasing and perfect.

11 Do not be slothful in zeal, but be burning
in spirit, serving the Lord.

_____
Date

Week 6 — Day 4   Today's verses

Psa. Behold, how good and how pleasant it is
133:1-2 for brothers to dwell in unity! It is like the
fine oil upon the head that ran down upon
the beard, upon Aaron's beard, that ran
down upon the hem of his garments.

Phil. For I know that for me this will turn out to
1:19 salvation through your petition and *the*
bountiful supply of the Spirit of Jesus Christ.

Date

Week 6 — Day 1   Today's verses

Deut. But to the place which Jehovah your God
12:5 will choose out of all your tribes to put His
name, to His habitation, shall you seek,
and there shall you go.

1 Cor. To the church of God which is in Corinth,
1:2 to those who have been sanctified in Christ
Jesus, the called saints, with all those who
call upon the name of our Lord Jesus Christ
in every place, *who is* theirs and ours.

Date

Week 6 — Day 5   Today's verses

Psa. Like the dew of Hermon that came down
133:3 upon the mountains of Zion. For there
Jehovah commanded the blessing: life forever.

1 Tim. And the grace of our Lord superabounded
1:14 with faith and love in Christ Jesus.

Rom. …Those who receive the abundance of
5:17 grace and of the gift of righteousness will
reign in life through the One, Jesus Christ.

Date

Week 6 — Day 2   Today's verses

Psa. For Jehovah has chosen Zion; He has de-
132:13-16 sired it for His habitation. This is My resting place forever; here will I dwell.…I will
abundantly bless its provision.…Its priests
I will clothe with salvation, and its faithful
ones will shout with a ringing shout.

133:1 Behold, how good and how pleasant it is
for brothers to dwell in unity!

Date

Week 6 — Day 6   Today's verses

John I in them, and You in Me, that they may be
17:23 perfected into one, that the world may know
that You have sent Me and have loved them
even as You have loved Me.

Psa. Bless Jehovah now, all you servants of Jeho-
134:1-3 vah who stand by night in the house of Jehovah. Lift up your hands in the sanctuary,
and bless Jehovah. May Jehovah, who made
heaven and earth, bless you from Zion.

Date

Week 6 — Day 3   Today's verses

Eph. Being diligent to keep the oneness of the
4:3-6 Spirit in the uniting bond of peace: one Body
and one Spirit, even as also you were called
in one hope of your calling; one Lord, one
faith, one baptism; one God and Father of
all, who is over all and through all and in all.

Date

Week 7 — Day 4   Today's verses

1 Cor. What then, brothers? Whenever you come
14:26 together, each one has a psalm, has a
teaching, has a revelation, has a tongue,
has an interpretation. Let all things be
done for building up.

Heb. Not abandoning our own assembling to-
10:25 gether, as the custom with some is, but
exhorting *one another*; and so much the
more as you see the day drawing near.

_____
Date

Week 7 — Day 5   Today's verses

2 Tim. For which cause I remind you to fan into
1:6-7 flame the gift of God, which is in you
through the laying on of my hands. For
God has not given us a spirit of cowardice,
but of power and of love and of sober-
mindedness.

_____
Date

Week 7 — Day 6   Today's verses

Eph. But holding to truth in love, we may grow
4:15-16 up into Him in all things, who is the
Head, Christ, out from whom all the
Body, being joined together and being
knit together through every joint of the
rich supply and *through* the operation in
the measure of each one part, causes the
growth of the Body unto the building up
of itself in love.

_____
Date

Week 7 — Day 1   Today's verses

Eph. And He subjected all things under His
1:22-23 feet and gave Him *to be* Head over all
things to the church, which is His Body,
the fullness of the One who fills all in all.

_____
Date

Week 7 — Day 2   Today's verses

John *Even the* Spirit of reality, whom the world
14:17 cannot receive, because it does not behold Him or know *Him; but* you know
Him, because He abides with you and
shall be in you.

Eph. One Body and one Spirit, even as also
4:4 you were called in one hope of your
calling.

_____
Date

Week 7 — Day 3   Today's verses

1 Cor. For even as the body is one and has many
12:12 members, yet all the members of the body,
being many, are one body, so also is the
Christ.

Eph. This mystery is great, but I speak with re-
5:32 gard to Christ and the church.

_____
Date

Week 8 — Day 4 — Today's verses

Col. And have put on the new man, which is
3:10-11 being renewed unto full knowledge according to the image of Him who created him, where there cannot be Greek and Jew, circumcision and uncircumcision, barbarian, Scythian, slave, free man, but Christ is all and in all.

_____
Date

Week 8 — Day 5 — Today's verses

Col. Greet the brothers in Laodicea, as well as
4:15-16 Nymphas and the church, which is in his house. And when this letter is read among you, cause that it be read in the church of the Laodiceans also, and that you also read the one from Laodicea.

_____
Date

Week 8 — Day 6 — Today's verses

Eph. And *that* you be renewed in the spirit of
4:23 your mind.

Rev. And the seventh angel trumpeted; and
11:15 there were loud voices in heaven, saying, The kingdom of the world has become the *kingdom* of our Lord and of His Christ, and He will reign forever and ever.

_____
Date

Week 8 — Day 1 — Today's verses

Eph. Abolishing in His flesh the law of the com-
2:15-16 mandments in ordinances, that He might create the two in Himself into one new man, *so* making peace, and might reconcile both in one Body to God through the cross, having slain the enmity by it.

_____
Date

Week 8 — Day 2 — Today's verses

Matt. While he was still speaking, behold, a
17:5 bright cloud overshadowed them, and behold, a voice out of the cloud, saying, This is My Son, the Beloved, in whom I have found My delight. Hear Him!

Col. And He is the Head of the Body, the
1:18 church; He is the beginning, the Firstborn from the dead, that He Himself might have the first place in all things.

_____
Date

Week 8 — Day 3 — Today's verses

Col. Which are a shadow of the things to come,
2:17 but the body is of Christ.

Gal. My children, with whom I travail again in
4:19 birth until Christ is formed in you.

_____
Date

Week 9 — Day 4   Today's verses

Gen. ...Jehovah God built the rib, which He had
2:22-24 taken from the man, into a woman and
brought her to the man. And the man said,
This time this is bone of my bones and flesh of
my flesh; this one shall be called Woman because out of Man this one was taken. Therefore a man shall leave his father and his
mother and shall cleave to his wife, and they
shall become one flesh.

_____
Date

Week 9 — Day 1   Today's verses

Jer. ...Thus says Jehovah: I remember concern-
2:2 ing you the kindness of your youth, the love
of your bridal days, when you followed after
Me in the wilderness...

Eph. ...Christ also loved the church and gave
5:25 Himself up for her.

27 That He might present the church to Himself glorious, not having spot or wrinkle or
any such things, but that she would be holy
and without blemish.

_____
Date

Week 9 — Day 5   Today's verses

John But one of the soldiers pierced His side
19:34 with a spear, and immediately there came
out blood and water.

36 For these things happened that the Scripture might be fulfilled: "No bone of His
shall be broken."

_____
Date

Week 9 — Day 2   Today's verses

Gen. And Jehovah God said, It is not good for the
2:18 man to be alone; I will make him a helper
as his counterpart.

22 And Jehovah God built the rib, which He
had taken from the man, into a woman
and brought her to the man.

_____
Date

Week 9 — Day 6   Today's verses

John He who has the bride is the bridegroom....
3:29-30 He must increase, but I *must* decrease.

Rev. And the Spirit and the bride say, Come! And
22:17 let him who hears say, Come! And let him
who is thirsty come; let him who wills take
the water of life freely.

_____
Date

Week 9 — Day 3   Today's verses

Gen. Now Jehovah God had formed from the
2:19-21 ground every animal of the field and every
bird of heaven. And He brought *them* to the
man to see what he would call them....But
for Adam there was not found a helper as his
counterpart. And Jehovah God caused a deep
sleep to fall upon the man, and he slept; and
He took one of his ribs and closed up the flesh
in its place.

_____
Date